The Mysteries of Medicinal Mushrooms~ Discover The Lifesaving Secrets

Michele Wildflower
HHP, CCC, RM

Dedication

I would like to dedicate this book to my daughters, my husband and all those who are seeking the truth. To those who don't know where to turn, who want to live a healthy life or who want to help a loved one feel better and to parents who want to educate themselves to protect their children.

With the knowledge of the material contained in this book, any discomfort or symptom should be alleviated. It is my gift to you so that you will know how to live your healthiest, most vibrant life enjoying the gifts you've been given with the knowledge of how to prepare the remedies from Mother Nature's Pantry if the time comes. If your loved one, don't give up! I compiled much of this for you. Knowledge Is Power.

"Never doubt that a small group of thoughtful, committed citizens can change the world; indeed, it's the only thing that ever has."

—Margaret Mead

Acknowledgements

First, I'd like to thank my husband, Iggy Wildflower, my best friend, who ignited the spark for my quest of seeking out natural alternatives to raise our girls by gifting me a Homeopathy Correspondence course for my 30th birthday. And for always standing by my side, learning with me, processing everything that comes into my reality and guiding me to make sense of it all, I couldn't have done this without your never ending, unconditional love and support.

I'd like to thank my four daughters: Marijah, Cherisse, Amareena and Isabel for giving me a reason to seek better alternatives. For showing me not only the amazing joy and love that only you could bring but for all that you've taught me and continue to teach me every day, I am so grateful.

I want to thank Dr. Paul Fanny of The University of Natural Health for asking me to write an Herbal Course, hence my book and the freedom to pass on my knowledge to the world in my own way.

And lastly, my patients and customers who trust me with their health, it is an honor to serve you and I appreciate all that you've taught me, this journey would not have been possible without your lessons and affirmations that I am on the right track.

Thank you, Everyone! ❤️

About the Author

Michele Wildflower has been fascinated by mushrooms her whole life, she loves foraging for them and has been utilizing mushroom medicine for almost a decade. She believes that they helped her to save her husband from a grim cancer diagnosis in 2016. Director of Education at Nature's Mysteries Academy of Holistic Health, Clinical Cannabinoid Clinician, Holistic Health Practitioner, Founder and Alchemist for Nature's Mysteries Apothecary, she offers classes and workshops available for large or small groups.

As a Homeopath, Herbalist, Reiki Master, Essential Oil Coach, Nutritionist, Certified in Complementary and Alternative Medicine, celebrating over 20 years in business, Michele is passionate about alternative medicine and loves to pass on the knowledge.

Other books Michele has written:

Discover The Essence Of Plant Medicine ~ The Five Principles Of Lifesaving Herbs
Discover The Essence Of Plant Medicine ~ The Five Principles Of Lifesaving Herbs Cannabis Edition
Herbs For Children ~A Parent's Guide To Blending Safe Herbal Remedies
Discover the Essence of Cannabis Medicine ~ The Lifesaving Principles (Coming Soon)

Understanding the importance of incorporating specific herbal compounds for certain symptom management to obtain overall health, Michele details the uses and properties of three different mushrooms she has used on her healing journey but also incorporates interesting fungi facts just for fun.

Cool mushroom I found.

"Mushrooms are the keys to the world's best-kept secrets."

—Paul Stamets

Table of Contents

Introduction

For those who are seeking answers whether to questions that they've wondered about or for remedies to a life threatening condition, the information contained herein will guide you on your path to optimum health.

I searched for answers when my husband was dying from Non Hodgkin's Lymphoma in 2016. Given only a 35% chance of curing it, I refused to believe that there was no hope. I spent tireless hours researching and thankfully found the perfect combination to save his life.

His whole story is included in the book. After reading about his diagnosis and the course of events that occurred, it is hoped that others with a cancer diagnosis will continue to fight and not give up knowing that there are safe remedies out there available. Included is how to prepare them as well.

There are no receptors in our body to receive from pharmaceutical medications, however supreme mushroom remedies nourish the body in more ways than one.

This is what we'll discover as we explore three different mushrooms~ Chag, Reishi and Turkey Tail, the conditions that they treat as well as the healing properties that they hold.

But before we get to the mysteries of the mushrooms, I'm assuming you want to know because there is some kind of condition, ailment or symptom that you are trying to treat.

While mushrooms can help to not only alleviate but cure many illnesses, there are many diseases that we suffer from that actually result from our own doing.

Before we can heal ourselves, it's imperative to understand what makes us sick, right?

So, we will explore some lifestyle choices that decrease immune function. Often, just removing that which hinders our immune function, results in well being.

Tracing back to the origins of herbal medicine and it's decline gives us a basis for understanding the pillars on which it stands and those who tried to tear it down. Knowing their shortcomings, enables us to rise above the propaganda and slander that has tried to undermine alternative practitioners' efforts.

Once our understanding is clear as to the manifestation of disease, we begin to uncover the ways to forage and then extract the healing compounds of medicinal mushrooms and how to treat ourselves with them. Examining the difference between prescribing and diagnosing becomes clear.

Uncover why mushrooms possess a whole host of benefits rather than a long list of side effects…

Chapter 1 ~ History And Background Of Herbs

In this chapter, we will begin to understand how long the relationship between humans and the fungi kingdom has lasted and how it has stood the test of time. A little history of herbs/mushrooms (I use them interchangeably as mushrooms are herbs) is included along with the background and basis for understanding the world of Holistic Herbal Healing and who the important founders of herbal medicine were.

Folk medicine will be understood, an understanding of how and when it shifted from natural herbal medicine to chemical medications is laid down as well as the underlying deceit that is the foundation of synthetic, chemical medications and the introduction to their own medical term for 'doctor induced disease'= Iatrogenic Disease…..

History

In the beginning herbs were the only form of medicine and herbal remedies were the medicine that was taught and used. Herbs have been used for 60,000 years. The oldest written herbal known is, *The Ebers Papyrus*, written around 1500 BCE, naming more than 125 herbs with over 800 prescriptions for poultices, salves, enemas, suppositories, pills, gargles, salves, inhalations, liquid medicines and directions for fumigation.

Epiduras was the first spa, founded in the sixth century BCE in Greece, by Aesculapius, the ancient Greek God of Medicine, son of the God, Apollo and the nymph Coronis, utilizing herbal decoctions, baths, fasting, sea breezes with fresh mountain air, along with the therapeutic use of drama, games and music.

The ruins can still be seen, including a large stone slab with famous cures from over 400 herbs inscribed into it. Thales of Miletus and Pythagoras of Samos compiled these 600 years later.

There were many other sanatoriums like the Epiduras throughout Greece who kept meticulous records of disease and treatments. Study of these records gave birth to the art of diagnosing and the study of the natural history of disease.

Folk Medicine

Folk medicine or the household use of herbal remedies was the first medicine and dates back to prehistoric times supporting many settled and traveling herbalists. In the fourth century BCE, Theophrastus wrote the Greek book that founded the science of Botany, *Historia Plantarum*.

We have the ancient monasteries to thank for diligently hand copying manuscripts from historic Greek and Roman texts when the Christian church preferred faith healing over the formal practice of medicine. The monasteries then became a local hub of medical knowledge; their luscious herb gardens provided the herbal remedies for most disorders.

If not the monasteries, folks turned to the 'wise women' of the village seeking their secret remedies of herbal lore passed down for generations including enchantments and spells. These were the 'wise women' who became the targets and victims of the hysteria of the Inquisitions and Witch Trials in the Middle Ages.

For example, if you take St. John's wort flowers and put them in olive oil or any other kind of oil and set that jar in front of a window, the liquid will turn red over a period of time, even though the flowers are yellow. This has nothing to do with witchcraft, sorcery or the Devil. This is a result of the substance found in the plant called Hypericin.

Hypericin is known to be a potent antiviral, antidepressant, antimicrobial, etc. Because of this compound changing the oil from yellow flowers to red meant the loss of many women's lives, it meant that these women were demons, possessed and working for and with the Devil, whom most of them didn't even acknowledge as he is within the Christian religion, which most of them weren't apart of and so they were called 'witches' and were executed. Sadly, many of the 9,000,000 women who were executed during the Witch Trials were Herbalists and women who knew the craft of herbs.

The anonymous *Grete Herball* of 1526 was the first Herbal to be published in English with two more following that are probably the two best known Herbals in English: the first in 1597 by John Gerard titled: *The Herbal or General History Of Plants* and then *The English Physician Enlarged* in 1653 by Nicholas Culpepper.

Enjoying phenomenal popularity despite being ridiculed by the peers of his day, mostly in retaliation for translating their Latin book of official medicines into English, Culpepper's blend of astrology, folklore, magic, and traditional medicine remained a favorite.

An herb in the Middle Ages might be prescribed by a peasant grandmother, sold by a traveling herbalist, charmed to be an ingredient in a magical potion or brew by a 'wise women' or quack, or pulverized into a repulsive and complex blend to be applied by a physician with hopes of bringing relief.

Otzi

Have you ever heard of Otzi? Discovered in 1991, scientists have confirmed he lived about 3300 BCE, he was found frozen in an alpine glacier in the Alps on the border of Italy and Austria, but the cool part is that he was carrying two species of mushrooms!

The Brich polypore was one, commonly used for fighting infections and the second was a tinder polypore also medicinal which can be used as firestarter, when pummeled into powder and then carried when traveling to keep warm.

Paracelsus

The downfall of herbal medicine began as early as the seventeenth century with the introduction by the physician Paracelsus of utilizing active chemical drugs such as arsenic, copper sulfate, iron, sulfur and mercury as healing substances.

Too bad his other beliefs corresponding to plants didn't stick. He believed that through the wise use of plants, whose properties correspond to their ruling planet, a beneficial astral influence would be directed into the body neutralizing disease.

He taught that there was a vital essence in all living things he called, 'mumia' and that the Universe was a manifestation of this life force which acted through differentiated forms.

Believing that food was an important factor contributing to man's health recognizing that spark in all living things, which is the opposite of physicians today, regarding the Universe as an accumulation of forms which can be considered separately and treated without regard for a unifying force.

Carnegie and Rockefeller

By the beginning of the twentieth century the herbal schools that were mainstream became the target or focus of attack by the medical profession preferring chemotherapy and other synthetic medications over herbal remedies.

The attack became so real, that doctors who practiced Herbal Medicine started becoming known as quacks. Dr. Ignaz Semmelweis was the first to think of washing hands before surgery and they called him a quack, too!

Prior to this, there were Herbal Schools and Homeopathic Schools as well as Eclectic Herbal Schools, the field of medicine was vast, there was not only one way to bring about healing. Various methods were employed and taught with outstanding results.

Around the turn of the last century, the Carnegie group and the Rockefeller group came together and decided that they wanted to 'reform' medical education in America. They wanted it to be the 'one way,' that is the single molecule, synthetically derived compounds that they were producing.

The way that they did this was by creating a medical monopoly and getting a hold of the education system to eliminate any competition to patent petrochemical medical education, hence the 'Flexnor Report' of 1910.

The Flexnor Report

This was a report by Abraham and Simon Flexnor, hired to do this preordained commissioned report. The foundation of the report was finding that it was far too easy to start a medical school and that most schools were not teaching sound medicine; meaning that the schools were not pushing enough medication that the Rockefellers and Carnegies were manufacturing.

The AMA, who were the evaluators of the medical colleges, made it their job to target and put an end to the larger respected Homeopathic colleges. Carnegie and Rockefeller began showering millions of dollars on these medical schools who were pushing their drug intensive patented medications.

After the donations to these universities, a consequence would be to have a member of their team on the school's Board of Directors 'just to ensure the money was being spent appropriately.' By loading up these Boards of Directors of specific teaching institutions with folks who were on the donor's payroll, the curriculums of these centers swung directly in the direction of pharmaceutical drugs having no emphasis on natural medicine, anymore.

Quackery or Conspiracy?

By 1925, over 10,000 Herbalists were out of business and by 1940 over 1500 Chiropractors would be prosecuted for practicing quackery. The 22 Homeopathic Medical Schools that were flourishing during the 1900's dwindled down to just 2 by 1923. By 1950, all the schools teaching Homeopathy were closed.

This made finding a job nearly impossible, if a physician hadn't graduated from a 'Flexnor Approved' school. Sound a little bit like a conspiracy?

As published in The New York Times in 1987 on August 29, four Chiropractors actually took the AMA to court for Conspiracy accusing them of having a branch within their organization designed to eliminate Chiropractic as a profession, which is and was then a licensed profession, through the use of propaganda. Judge Susan Getzendanner found them guilty of conspiracy. You can look it up yourself - Wilk versus the AMA court ruling of 1987.

This explains why the whole medical field has been skewed and so focused on single molecule, money making, side effecting medicine. Unfortunately, it is all about the money and not healing anymore. In medical school, the amount of time spent on nutrition is minimal with the majority of time spent on learning various pharmaceutical medications and how to use them.

Not saying that all doctors are misguided, there are many amazing doctors out there doing a lot of good! But the underlying history of the profession and the motivation behind it has been, let's say, questionable, to say the least.

Chemotherapy

Chemotherapy was originally inspired by mustard gas and was actually a result of investigations that were done after the war, in the early 1940s when they dropped nitrogen mustard gas in Italy. In the post mortem autopsies they could see that the lymphocytes of these patients had dropped down.

For people with leukemia or lymphoma where the lymphocytes are producing too much, doctors had the idea that because they were suppressed in the patients who were victims of mustard gas, mustard gas could be used as a treatment.

In a study, 90% of physicians said they would not prescribe chemotherapy for their wife or their children. Utilizing the most toxic substances known to man that damage the internal organs, not just kill cancer, so that even after the cancer is gone, a patient is left with resounding or life threatening even, side effects such as damage to their heart valve, leaky gut, ulcers, breathing problems, neuropathy, chemo brain, loose teeth, bone pain, secondary cancers that are more virile than the primary cancer, etc.

After 5 years of chemo, there's only a 2.1% survival rate. In a study done by Epidemiologists who themselves were doctors, they found that 90% of people who underwent chemotherapy treatments died within 5 years of treatment. This study was published in the 2004 edition of the Journal of Oncology.

Damaging DNA, chemo and radiation have a very high propensity to create secondary cancers. Which is why they do not say you are cured until you are 5 years out, otherwise, they call it remission, fully expecting it to come back. A good indication of the toxicity is the fact that they have to suit up to administer it to you.

Iatrogenic Disease

Iatrogenic disease is a term used to describe doctor induced illness. Can you believe there is actually a medical 'term' or 'diagnosis' for what we should basically be calling malpractice?

Only 42-46% of cancer patients die from Cachexia, which is from the actual cancer which would be from losing all of their lean body mass. Which means that what kills the majority of cancer patients is pneumonia, liver failure, kidney failure, sepsis, etc. which are mostly all associated with chemotherapy and radiation treatment.

Epigenetics

Epigenetics is the science of gene expression. No one is condemned to poor health because of their genes. Epigenetics proves to us that through nutrients, intention and thoughtful dedicated action we can change our gene expression.

This means that we are not bound by the choices our ancestors made, we are forging our own path, for our own health, for our own destiny. Nothing is predestined by the faults of our ancestors.

But what happened, anyway? Why is it that 1 in 4 people will get cancer, these statistics are very different than they were 100 years ago. For starters, our grandparents grew most of their food, there was not all of the refined food choices that we have now, there was not all of the chemical pesticides and fertilizers that there are now. The destruction of our food supply began over 50 years ago, which is a subject for another book.

See Discover The Essence Of Plant Medicine, The Five Principles Of Lifesaving Herbs for a complete summary of the downfall of our food supply.

Summary~

In this chapter, we explored the periods of time and influential figures in the world of herbs. The thousands of herbs that have been recorded over time by a number of Herbalists and scholars would not have made it into our pharmacopoeia had it not been for them.

We have them to thank for had it not been for them taking the time to record their results from each herb over a millennia, much of that ancient knowledge would have been lost. Now let's get into the mushroom mysteries…

Chapter 2 ~ The Ancient Link/Our Future Hope

"Beneath the forest floor, mushrooms are exchanging information, making connections."

—Unknown

In this chapter, we'll explore the ancient connection we have with mushrooms and the ways in which they heal our bodies, we'll have a deeper understanding of the mycelium under our feet and the 'world wide web' of roots, hyphae and mycelium connecting every plant and fungi species growing in the forest.

We'll grasp the mutual exchange of vital compounds for each one's survival and the complementary relationship of nutrient transportation between roots from one species to another.

We'll consider the idea of pollution eating mushrooms, yes, you heard that correctly!

The Ancient Link

When the dinosaurs were wiped out and there was nothing but destruction on the Earth's surface, this was when fungi took over the Earth, so to speak. Thriving on decaying matter, their bounty was full.

If it wasn't for fungi, our world would be full of decaying matter. Mushrooms are the ones who break it down it for us. In a sense, they make life from death.

The ancient link between us and fungi is apparent within our bodies, deep within our cells where we have receptors to receive immune modulating effects from them.

When we ingest mushrooms, there is an ancient recognition according to Christopher Hobbs, 4th generation Herbalist. The interaction between our cells is ancient.

It's kind of an awakening within our gut reaching ancient immune receptor sites.

Ten of our most valuable medicines are derived from fungi, mushrooms are the missing link for chronic disease sufferers.

Scientists predict that there's somewhere between 4 and 5 million species of fungi on the planet with only 200, 000 documented. There's so much we don't know about these amazing gifts from Nature.

It is thought that we've only uncovered about 5% of all of the fungi species on Earth.

According to Christopher Hobbs, who I mentioned prior, upon closer inspection into fungi DNA, research has shown that mushrooms are more closely related to animals than plants.

Per the Doctrine of Signatures, when mushrooms are sliced you will see the resemblance to a human ear, they serve as one of the few foods that contain vitamin D, which has been found to improve hearing and is important for healthy bones, including the tiny ones in your ear that transmit sound to the brain.

Coincidence or synchronicity? I'll have to go with synchronicity!

A Beautiful Dance

Mycorrhiza (mycro=fungus, rhiza= root) is a symbiotic relationship between plants, specifically their roots and fungi in the soil. When this relationship occurs, the plant becomes a 'host' to the fungi.

This relationship has a lot to do with the health of the plant, the nutrients coming in and how the plant synthesizes it. The fungi live in the roots of the plant, sends out filaments called hyphae or threadlike elements that spread from the root of the plant creating a living, connected network in the soil called mycelium.

Able to sense the world, even though they have no eyes or nose, they can sense light, smell chemicals, feel heat, detect electricity. Always collecting information for decision making in the process of where to go grow or what chemicals to make next. Proving that a brain is not needed to solve problems.

By attaching to the root and spreading, it increases the available nutrients for the plant giving it a larger area to acquire nutrients from. The fungi receive sugar synthesized by the plant, in return.

The hyphae and bacteria, secreting a glue-like substance that improves soil structure and soil nutrient retention is part of what makes this relationship so complementary.

A beautiful dance goes on under the ground in our soil including microorganisms connecting, feeding off of each other in a kind of sustainable circle of interdependency, increasing the vitality of our plants.

Even stone cannot stop the hyphae. They utilize pressure that is 100x greater than inside of a car tire to break through rocks to feed on minerals.

In this way they can turn rock to life, like molecular mining.

Fungi is similar to the circulatory system of our planet.

The mycelium have more networks than we have neural pathways.

Mushrooms are the fruit of the fungus and the mycelium is the body of the fungus.

It is estimated that over 90% of plants rely on fungi to survive, with hundreds of kilometers of mycelial networks weaving under each foot.

Through these networks connecting all of the trees and plants, resources can be carried through the roots to one species of plant to another.

They are capable of growing to intense sizes, creating elaborate structures.

Known to have thrived on every continent.

There's even a species known as *Lactarius* deliciosus or Delicious Milkcap because when you break off a piece, it actually starts to ooze a liquid very similar looking to breast milk. This mushroom grows in North East India.

In Tasmania, where rainforests have existed for over sixty five million years, some of the most ancient fungi exist, including new species that we may not even be aware of.

This explains the urgency in ensuring we're utilizing organic methods when growing our own or as a consumer not only for ourselves but for the planet as well.

Mushrooms To The Rescue!

But our mushroom allies aren't only providing the necessary nutrients to keep our soil healthy, they may also be the answer to repairing the damage that has already been done to the planet in the form of pollution, specifically plastics.

Studies in China, where over 6000 different mushroom species can be found. Some of the oldest known fossils of fungi on the planet have been found in a specific region known as Yunnan Province.

Researchers have located a plastic eating fungus!

The ability of mushrooms to adapt to their environment in a short amount of time is also a good indicator of their divine intelligence.

Reproduction

Mushrooms, the organ of sexual reproduction for the fungus, release spores instead of seeds like a plant.

Releasing zillions of spores into the atmosphere. They are literally everywhere, every breath we take is full of spores.

Some release spores through the top of the mushroom and some release them from underneath.

These spores are so minute that it would take 25,000 of them to cover a pinhead.

If all those spores were to grow, the spores that just one gill released would produce over 5 miles of mushrooms!

Carrying genes, the spores are extremely lightweight and tiny.. when bugs eat mushrooms, they are actually helping to spread spores as well.

It seems mushrooms have symbiotic relationships with many different species.

Mushroom Prints

If you take a mushroom with gills underneath and remove the stem, lay it on a piece of paper and wait a few hours, you will see a mushroom print!

The print is made up of 10's of 1000's of microscopic spores.

Beta Glucans

One of the most beneficial compounds found in medicinal mushrooms are beta-glucans.

They are a type of soluble fiber in the form of a helix, an integral part of the cell walls of mushrooms.

About 55% of Reishi cell walls are made up of beta glucans.

Beta glucans supercharge our macrophage, the ones who seek out and destroy invaders enabling us to fight cancer and other abnormal cells as well as any pathogens within the body upregulating our immune system.

But that's not all, they also improve blood pressure and cholesterol levels, improve blood glucose control protecting against insulin resistance/type 2 diabetes according to Dr. Axe as well as helping to support immune function, treating skin conditions, reducing the risk of obesity due to increasing satiety while decreasing fatigue that is caused by an immune function with decreased immune function or emotional/physical stress.

Summary~

In this chapter, we recognize how old fungi is and the ancient link that connects us to mushroom medicine, with the knowing of the beautiful dance taking place underneath our feet.

Uncovering just how many species there are and how they have contributed to modern medicine is realized.

We have hope of a future with less plastic waste thanks to a plastic eating fungus!

Chapter 3 ~ Foraging, Drying And Storage

Chaga from my woods that I haven't harvested, just visit.

"Mushrooms were the roses in the garden of that unseen world because the real mushroom plant was underground. The parts you could see — what most people called a mushroom —was just a brief apparition. A cloud flower."

—*Margaret Atwood*

In this chapter, we'll compare the differences between foraging and harvesting, as well as proper foraging etiquette.

We're reminded of the importance of locally harvested medicine and of the astrological influences at play and how we can utilize and harness these subtle energies ensuring the integrity and vitality of our mushrooms.

Why the propert identification guide can save your life is understood as well as the basics of Biodynamic inoculation, foraging and harvesting.

Foraging or Harvesting?

It is thought that there are over 2000 edible mushrooms and 300 species have medicinal properties. Whether we're looking for food or medicine, foraging for mushrooms is one of my favorite pastimes!

Mushroom lovers looking for mushrooms for personal use is foraging, mushroom harvesting is commercial, large scale harvesting which often results in overharvesting.

Always leave at least half to grow back for next year.

Different species of mushrooms grow in different places on specific tree species. Before you head out, confirm which tree species the mushroom that you are looking for is growing.

Bring a basket (so the spores fall out as you walk) and a sharp knife.

Make sure that you don't need any permits. Ensure that you are not harvesting endangered mushroom species, right? Check your local laws before you forage.

Always properly identify the mushroom that you're foraging as some species can be deadly.

It is imperative that your identification guide is not ai generated as they are not always accurate and considering some species are lethal, refer to a reputable source, someone like Paul Stamets who actually discovered a species of mushroom that we had not previously known existed.

Minimize the damage to the surrounding area, meaning that you are not stomping on and killing all of the surrounding flora. Just try to be mindful and responsible and respectful, which I know you will because you're taking the time to learn now. Ever heard the saying, 'leave no trace?'

There are very particular ways to forage mushrooms when removing them from their base, so please refer to a guide with specific foraging guidelines for the mushroom you're searching for. For example, Paul Stamets, who I mentioned previously recommends never pulling them out of the ground, always cutting with a sharp knife so that they continue to grow.

Biodynamics

I prefer to forage according to Biodynamic rhythms, as the moon travels through the sky and crosses into and through the various constellations. If attention is paid as to its placement when foraging and drying mushrooms, then the optimum potential of the mushroom can be reached.

Plants correlate with one of these signs and elements, depending on what part you are using. Mushrooms are not plants, however…

- **Leaves** correlate with the **water** element and the signs of **Pisces, Cancer, Scorpio**

- **Flowers** correlate with the **air** element and the signs of **Aquarius, Gemini, Libra**

- **Fruit** correlates with the **fire** element and the signs of **Aries, Leo, Sagittarius**

- **Roots** correlate with the **earth** element and the signs of **Taurus, Virgo, Capricorn**

For a study into inoculating mushrooms according to Biodynamic rhythms, see https://aztro1.com/research/biodynamic-mushroom-farming.htm.

In this double blind research performed at a mushroom farm, it was revealed that yields were the highest from mushrooms inoculated on Air and Fire days.

Water days were the poorest yields.

This makes sense when you think of the spores being released into the air, similar to flower's essence (terpenes) being released into the air.

Also, the fact that the Fire days results were higher than others would validate the theory of the mushroom being the fruit of the fungi.

Foraging while observing cosmic rhythms ensures the quality of your mushrooms due to the unseen astrological influences at play.

Mushrooms foraged this way last longer and retain their color longer than others that weren't.

The Strongest Looking

When foraging, care should be taken as to which are the strongest if being used for medicine. These will be the first choice.

Do not choose mushrooms that do not look vibrant and healthy.

Scrawny, mildewed, yellowing, unhealthy mushrooms that are suffering from lack of light or inadequate nutrients or display signs of infestation or any other signs of disease would definitely not be ideal medicine.

Local

Always begin with mushrooms in your area. By utilizing local mushrooms that were grown in similar conditions to where you live, these will contain compounds that your body can utilize to boost your immune system.

Much the same as the idea that using local honey decreases the likelihood of allergies developing. Wild mushrooms are always the best choice for herbal medicines.

Although this isn't always possible depending on the season or locale where you are looking. As a rule, wild mushrooms have more and sometimes even rare curative properties compared to their cultivated counterparts, which loses some rare medicinal values that they possess when grown in the wild in its natural growing environment.

Serenity

Consider factors when foraging such as powerlines, traffic, road proximity, neighbors (nuclear power plant, cell towers.)

Mushrooms growing in a forest will be purer than the ones growing next to the road which is maintained with salt in the winter and herbicides and pesticides for the grass in the summer. The importance of purity in your formulations cannot be stressed enough.

When foraging, take note as to which locations have the healthiest sites and when it is the optimum harvest time.

I always thank the mushroom when harvesting and never take the whole patch, bringing an offering is always a nice thought, too.

If you are purchasing mushrooms, under what conditions were they foraged or grown? Near a city? Or out in the country where there is hopefully no smog, less emissions, purer water quality, cleaner air, etc. These are questions you want answers to.

Organic

Not all mushrooms are the same. By choosing organic, we are making a conscious choice to incorporate unadulterated fungi in its purest form without the use of carcinogenic pathogens that hide in plain sight, under a cloak labeled pesticides and fertilizers.

For example, they say carrots are high in vitamin A, right? Oranges are high in vitamin C, but if these plants were grown under toxic conditions in depleted vitamin void soil, then how much vitamin A or vitamin C is the plant really going to contain?

Compare this to a plant that is grown in vital soil full of the necessary components to guarantee plant nutrition, and that is balanced by all of the microorganisms in the soil feeding off of each other.

Drying

Drying mushrooms can either be done by air drying, in a dehydrator, or with heat. If needed immediately, the mushroom can be placed in the oven on the lowest temperature for 20 minutes or until dry. Although this isn't ideal, it can work.

Making sure to keep the mushrooms below 140 degrees F is essential to preserve potent nutritional and medicinal properties.

While also ensuring that mushrooms reach a temperature that's effective at killing any eggs that insects may have laid in the mushroom.

For air drying, mushrooms can be hung or laid out on a screen with plenty of room around each mushroom.

If screens are being utilized, turn mushrooms every day. Drying mushrooms in sunlight actually increases their vitamin D content!

After mushrooms are dry, freezing them is a great method for preventing long term problems with storage due to insect damage.

Storing

Dried mushrooms can be stored, ideally in a paper bag or glass jar, plastic bags can be used but care should be used ensuring that they are BPA free. Don't want to defeat your purpose storing them in plastic which has known carcinogens or cancer-causing chemicals present.

Dried mushrooms can be stored in a cool, dark place or in the freezer.

This is my ideal choice to ensure freshness.

As stated, paper bags are another option. There are even paper bags with roll tops that have a little window in the front so you can see your mushrooms, some have a BPA-free lining inside.

Glass jars are also another option, but care needs to be taken that mushrooms are dried as thoroughly as possible; condensation can result in molding of your medicine.

Mushrooms should never be kept or stored or prepared near or in a microwave. As medicine, they should never be stored near electrical devices or cell phones, Wi-Fi routers, etc.

About the photo at the beginning of this chapter, I have always heard that Chaga grows in cones but before this day, I had never seen it. And I've seen a lot of Chaga growing in the woods, but it's NEVER in a cone.

My sources were reputable so it's not like I didn't believe them, but I had just never seen it, that's all. Didn't mean it didn't exist.

On this day in the photo, I was walking through my woods behind my house in the North East Kingdom of Vermont when I saw this TOTAL cone shaped Chaga mushroom growing!

I was so excited to not only find one but on my own property. I definitely didn't harvest it, I actually can see from the driveway that I walk up when I take my dogs for a walk. Whenever I go by, I just kind of look and wave and say,' hi Chaga!'

Summary~

Now you have a basic understanding of the difference between foraging and harvesting, what to look for when foraging and what's important to avoid as well as how to dry and store mushrooms.

We're reminded of the importance of locally harvested medicine and of the astrological influences at play and how we can utilize and harness these subtle energies ensuring the integrity and vitality of our mushrooms.

And now we will explore the best methods for extracting the beneficial compounds that these ancient remedies carry.

He's (She's) Gone "After Mushrooms"! poem by Boris Pasternak, poet and author of Doctor Zhivago. (Courtesy of MadAboutMushrooms.com)

The highway. Ditches. Woods.
We wander off in light
After mushrooms, and we mark
The mileposts left and right.

We leave the open highway.
We scatter, ranging through
The forest gloom; we ramble
Ankle-deep in dew.

Through thickets deep in dark
The spears of sunlight rush
On brown and yellow mushrooms
Under every bramblebush.

They hide among the stumps
Where birds alight to rest,
And when we lose ourselves,
The shadows guide our quest.

So brief these autumn days
And sunset solitudes,
The twilight has no chance
To linger in the woods.

Our bags and baskets burst
With gathered stock before
We leave for home: pine mushrooms
Make almost half our store.

Behind our backs the dark
Still forest walls arise,
And, beautiful in death,
The day flames bright and dies.

Sincere thanks to Librarian Midge Hayes of the Port Orford Library for tracking down this poem. It is reproduced on this website through the courtesy of University of Colorado, Boulder, CO 80309

Translated from the Russian by Eugene M. Kayden

Boris Pasternak: Poems

Second Edition, Revised and Enlarged

The Antioch Press, Yellow Springs, Ohio 1964, LCCN: 63-14379, Pages 244-245

Chapter 4 ~ Extraction Methods

2021~ My 4 Mushroom Double Extraction with Chaga, Turkey Tail, Shitake and Reishi

"The art of healing comes from nature, not from the physician. Therefore the physician must start from nature with an open mind."

—Paracelsus

In this chapter, we will explore the timeless art of extraction and ways to ensure that you retain as many of the valuable healing properties that mushrooms possess.

We will understand that there is not one way to extract mushroom compounds, this education is required in understanding specific methods for each different mushroom.

Introducing the idea that what you're thinking at the time of preparation can increase the efficacy of your remedy. The understanding of the capacity of water to store information will be introduced.

A basic understanding of what the Simpler's Method of Measurements is understood.

Extraction

Extraction is the art of drawing the healing compounds found in mushrooms into a carrier such as alcohol, water or vegetable glycerin. By removing the fiber and releasing only the beneficial components found in the mushroom, bypassing all of the waste, direct application of those fortifying compounds can be achieved without the effort of digestion which can steal the bodies energy away from healing during critical moments when the location of the available energy the body has is crucial, allowing it to direct itself into healing as opposed to the fires of digestion.

Because of the multitude of compounds found in mushrooms, the method of extraction can be critical to the viability of your medicine. If through the extraction process, you are eliminating all or any of the potent benefits, then you are defeating your purpose.

Extraction Methods

Because mushrooms have so many valuable compounds, a double extraction process is required to harness all of the beneficial compounds.

Preparations~

Because some of the active compounds that are present are not soluble in water such as the terpenes and sterols, a double extraction process is required with mushrooms.

First an alcohol extraction, then a decoction to release any compounds not released into the alcohol extraction, such as the polysaccharides, beta glucans and proteoglycans.

While Chaga can be made into tea, many of the potent benefits are lost without an alcohol extraction. The double extraction method described would be first choice for medicinal property extraction from Chaga. **

Double Extraction Method

Alcohol Tincture:

For mushrooms, alcohol is the preferred medium over glycerin…

Fill jar half way with dried mushroom

Cover with organic grain alcohol

Cap, label, shake everyday infusing with healing intention, love and gratitude.

After 1 month strain.

Decoction:

Place alcohol soaked mushrooms in a pot, cover with twice the amount of water.

1 part chopped up mushroom.

2 parts hot water using triple the amount of water used for the tincture.

Simmer on low heat for 2 to 6 hours.

Water will reduce quite a bit, add more as needed

Cool, compost mushrooms

Add equal parts decoction to equal parts alcohol tincture giving you a 25% alcohol extract if the alcohol was 100 proof (50% alcohol, 50% water).

Cap, shake well, label.

Standard Dose:

½ teaspoon two to three times a day.

Recipes are also included on each mushroom profile.

Tea Preparation:

Beverage:

1 tsp. herbs

1 cup of water

depending on the plant -

might be necessary to cover during the steeping process to ensure no loss of volatile oils.

But if we are using tea as medicine, larger quantities of herbs would be added. Making these blends in quart jars and having them on hand is easier than having to make a fresh cup every time for treatments where herbs are being administered throughout the day.

Medicinal:
1 tbs. herbs
1 cup water or
Steep for hours or overnight for stronger remedy
Strain, pour into sterilized jar, label.

Intention

Perhaps one of the most important steps in blending your mushroom remedy is your state of mind. If you are upset with someone or someone has wronged you in some way and you can't stop thinking about it, this is not the time to formulate medicine.

When you are creating your herbal formulas, it is imperative that you are thinking healing thoughts, in a happy frame of mind, without the interference of a TV playing some drama or crime show, hateful music, violent video games, toxic people, hateful people, etc.

A somewhat healing environment needs to be created and that's not to say that if you have children, they shouldn't be around or ANYTHING like that. Children have a high vibration.

What I'm saying is when you are gathering and creating your formulations, you want to have your intention set on healing, imagining the outcome you are striving for, extreme health. If it's for someone specific, imagine them whole, happy and healthy the whole time while you are preparing it, you can even repeat that while you are formulating it as well as healing thoughts such as, 'I feel better,' 'I grow stronger every day,' 'I enjoy vital health,' and any others that you might think of.

Imagining white light pouring into your formulations from above and filling them with Universal Healing Energy will also potentialize your remedy.

What you wouldn't want to do is think my pain is going away, my pain is gone, my pain has subsided. Every word has a vibration or frequency associated with it, in accordance with The Law of Attraction, we attract that which we focus on. So, we don't want to keep saying pain, or whatever it is that we don't want over and over, we want to say what we do want over and over.

Imagining the desired outcome will ensure the potency of your medicine.

Water's Secret

In Germany, in the 1960s, in a closed laboratory, one of the assistants dropped a vacuum sealed envelope of virulent poison into a vessel of distilled water. She left it there trying to conceal her mistake, three days later it was noticed.

Still sealed, no harm done. They gave this water to laboratory mice and the mice died. Tested immediately, results showed chemically, it was impeccably clean, meaning that somehow the water without direct contact with the poison somehow adopted its properties. Implying that somehow it received negative information from the poison.

A fantastic hypothesis was put forward to explain water's unpredictable behavior - water has memory. It records and stores information. There has been much research done over the last 50+ years proving this to be true.

The Simpler's Method of Measurements

While there are some folks who are very specific and meticulous in measuring their formulations, there are others who aren't, using a little bit of this and a pinch of that. Whichever way resonates with you is the way to go.

The Simpler's Method breaks recipes into parts instead of cups or ounces or grams. In this way, any herbal recipe can be enjoyed in a cup or on a larger scale.

Instead of using cups or ounces, measurements are converted into parts:

- two parts Reishi

- one part Chaga
- three parts Turkey Tail

The Simpler's Method suggests using large quantities of local, mild herbs continuously over a period of time.

Purity

When heating water for decoctions never use aluminum pots as they can leach into your medicine, never boil ingredients, never use a microwave or pour hot liquids into plastic.

Never use scratched Teflon for heating herbal concoctions (or any other time!)

Make sure to choose organic vodka, grain alcohol, glycerin, etc. when making preparations.

Only using fresh spring water, never fluoridated, chlorinated tap water should be used in preparations.

Glass measuring cups and pots are always the first choice when preparing your formulations, as well as metal measuring spoons, instead of plastic.

Plastic really has no place in an apothecary.

Labeling

The value that labeling holds is priceless. You might think that there is no way that you could possibly forget what's in that jar, but overtime, especially if you are an avid Herbalist with lots of concoctions... just save yourself the time and mental anguish of desperately trying to remember which jar was which. Not that this has EVER happened to me before, I can just imagine the dilemma before you. 'Ha ha - way too many times!'

You would think you'd learn after 30 years, but some habits die hard. Just label it and save yourself the guesswork. Use your brain power for creating new formulations not trying to remember what the old ones are.

Summary~

In this chapter, we learned the different techniques of extraction that have been used for longer than we can actually perceive. We're beginning to grasp the connectedness of creation.

By now, we understand the concept that what we think actually affects the world around us.

 We can now utilize an ancient technique when measuring our herbal formulations.

We have a clear picture of the differences between the various extraction methods and understand the reasoning behind them.

We know that the effects of microwave radiation on our medicine is undesirable, we know how vitally important it is to keep it and cell phones as far away from our herbal apothecary and the remedies contained within as possible. We understand what a waste of our time it would be to not just label it after we make it (learning from my mistakes).

2022 Alcohol Mushroom Extraction

Chapter 5 ~ Applications And Uses

2021~ Mushrooms Before Extraction

"It is far more important to know what person the disease has than what disease the person has."

—Hippocrates

In this chapter, a basic understanding of the importance of stabilization, detoxification and rebuilding and how these methods apply in all situations and is a foundational basis to start your treatment will be given. The Herxheimer Effect will be identified.

The Law of Opposites will be explored as well as an emphasis on research and safety when working with our mushroom allies. Grasping the toxicity of the diagnostic tests offered is imperative in making our own health decisions.

A foundation will be laid as to the beauty of Herbal Medicine and the dangers of Black Box Warnings and we'll find out what the leading cause of death in the US is. The dangers of NSAIDS will be investigated as well as the benefits of Energy Medicine and how your thoughts play into not only your personality, your everyday life, but your future as well.

We will learn some of the underlying causes of disease that might not be apparent and remedies to rectify those imbalances.

Prescribing not Diagnosing

First, let's remember that we are not treating a disease - we are treating a person. We are not trying to diagnose. In the end, all diagnoses are just 'terms' that have been used to describe a variety of symptoms, with the exception of cancer. Ultimately, each disease just boils down to 'dis-ease' in the body, including cancer.

We are trying to target specific symptoms and imbalances within the body and restore harmony within the system by moving energy, removing stagnation, nourishing the organs, stimulating circulation, flushing the lymph system, etc.

While some are writing prescriptions containing foreign molecules, we turn not to synthetic molecules but to molecules that the body knows how to synthesize. 'Synthesis over synthetic.'

No Isolated Symptoms

We are asking what else is going on besides an isolated symptom? There is never an isolated symptom unless it is the very beginning of disease. The majority of the time, there was something leading up to the illness.

If it's an acute (short term) condition such as a cold or congestion, then not much background is necessary; but for chronic ailments (cancer, emphysema) the root of the cause of dysfunction needs to be located so that it can be removed and then corrected.

Stabilize, Detoxify, Rebuild

Stabilization

With just about any issue the body is experiencing, we need to stabilize its condition, so the body is in a state of homeostasis in which the systems are maintaining stability and functioning properly.

We must decrease symptoms enough to manage diet upkeep, begin medicinal tea administration and any compresses or poultices that are needed.

Often illness and disease can be a result of an accumulation of toxins in the system, which require elimination. If the patient is too weak or not strong enough to remove them on their own, then the body needs assistance detoxifying. In this case the first job is to stabilize the condition so that treatment can begin and have efficient absorption.

Once the body is stable enough to keep liquids down, nourishing teas can start being administered to build strength. In this state, the patient can relax, eat and conduct themselves without displaying too many symptoms or enduring extreme weakness.

Detoxify

The next objective is detoxification. The body can only withstand so much before it starts experiencing difficulties in managing its normal daily functions. Limit exposure.

With too many toxins being introduced, the body becomes stressed and pressured, once you can stabilize it, with the proper nutrients and support needed, it is time to start slowly detoxifying to remove as many of those toxic components as possible.

Herxheimer Effect or the Healing Crisis

Start detox. As the toxins are eliminated, the individual could feel worse before better, the importance of detoxifying slowly cannot be stressed enough.

This is called Herxheimer Effect or the Healing Crisis.

•   If cancer is the condition being treated, as cancer cells die they accumulate in the blood which can cause an ill feeling.

•   If not cancer, the toxins recirculating in the blood as they are removed before they are fully processed by the liver can induce an unpleasant sensation.

During this time the body is detoxing, during this detox, the blood has many toxins running through it causing a variety of symptoms until those compounds are absorbed and processed by the liver.

During this detoxing healing process, it is normal for the patient to not feel good and sometimes perhaps even feel worse before they feel better. If this is the case then slow down the detox.

While it is a reality, it is not necessary. If the patient does not feel good, decrease the quantity or frequency of intervals of administration to slow down the detox and give the body time to process the toxins. Some people say it's necessary, but I don't believe in making patients feel worse than they already do even though it's for a good cause.

Slowing down the detox process is sometimes more necessary in my opinion than the patient enduring the Healing Crisis.

Distilled Water

Drinking lots of distilled water with a pinch of sea salt attracts impurities from within the body like a magnet and has cleansing properties as well. Oftentimes, detoxification and removing as many toxins as possible in the immediate environment can alleviate many symptoms. After the detox protocol is completed, then beginning to strengthen the body with nervine mushrooms that build the internal organs can begin.

Rebuilding

This is a vital component in restoring energy and in supporting the growth of new cells. Getting enough rest, in the dark, connecting with our Higher Power, The Universe, Buddha, Allah, God once a day and filling our bodies full of healing love and energy, plenty of exercise, taking vitamins, enzymes, mushrooms, juicing fresh organic veggies, drinking fresh organic smoothies and toning teas, restoring healthy flora in the gut, maintaining a healing atmosphere, are all THINGS that we can do, that will not only give them more time, whether it's a pet or person, but will increase their quality of life.

Treatment

Mushrooms work synergistically together and can be combined in most formulations.

Finding the perfect balance of ingredients can sometimes be the tricky part but this is where trial and error comes in. Other herbs can be added or the amount of herbs can be increased or the frequency of administration can be increased.

Think of the symptoms you are trying to treat. Which one is the most important, or the worst, or causing the harshest symptoms?

I would start there, researching herbs to bring relief, then supplement with other herbs that can address symptom management.

One method of practice is to target symptoms or a condition and utilize as many of those herbs listed for treating those symptoms in your formulations as possible.

The Beauty of Herbal Plant Medicine

The beauty of herbs is the ability to practice trial and error and not jeopardize one's life. In low doses, herbs are safe and can be slightly increased if the desired effect is not achieved.

Immediate results should not be expected though. If there's no sign of improvement after 3 days, reevaluate treatment. Oftentimes, relief can be achieved with mild herbs in large doses with herbal teas for acute conditions but for chronic conditions, sometimes long-term treatment is necessary with stronger herbs.

Sometimes a break in between doses is necessary to let the body function on its own for a week or two and then continue treatment due to the cumulative effects of the herbs on the system, over time.

Intuition

The role that intuition plays in herbal medicine is the vital link that was lost. The knowledge that wasn't passed down. The inclination that only our gut can give us.

That ancient part of us, the instinctual connection we have to Spirit or Mother Earth that whispers in our ear in a tiny, little mushroom voice, pick me! It's me, I am the chosen one. I can help restore health and vitality.

I cannot stress enough the importance of effective research. Always listen to yourself, if you feel the information you are receiving is not accurate, research it instead of believing everything that you hear or read.

When my husband was about to start his first five day long chemo treatments that he was scheduled to have every three weeks for three months, I asked the team of Oncologists at Dartmouth if there was anything that they could suggest to make the impact of the chemo easier on his system when they informed us of all of the side effects: nausea, vomiting, headaches, bone pain, joint pain, neuropathy, etc.

Their reply was that it's all how you go into it. If you think, *this is going to be the end of me* it will be. For patients who think, *I'm going to beat this and not let it take me down*, they will have fewer side effects.

This was great information coming from a doctor, that your thoughts play a crucial role in your recovery, which was great for my husband to hear this from someone other than myself. But at the same time I knew there had to be some herbs that we could incorporate to relieve some of the side effects on a physical level too.

I wasn't really sure which ones exactly but I knew enough to know that Turkey Tail would probably be one to boost his immune system.

And I could think of others for nausea but I didn't really have any first-hand experience with chemo or cancer. I said to my husband, "I just need to research it and see if there's some herb like Astragalus (of which I had never worked with before) that would help increase your white blood cells and ease the side effects."

Like I said Astragalus was not an herb that I had any experience with and I don't even know why I said it. But in my research, it turned out that it was a powerful ally to have on our side. I learned that it is used in Asia, given to patients who are undergoing chemo treatments.

Why did it pop into my head? That, I can't explain, but it was one of the best herbs for the remedy we were seeking at the time. So, sometimes intuition plays a vital role in the best herbal allies chosen for a particular treatment.

Remember to listen to yourself! If a mushroom pops into your mind when you think of a specific ailment, symptom or person, that is unfamiliar to you, research its properties. It may turn out to be your wisest choice for a specific ailment or a welcome addition to your preparation.

Other Factors

Sometimes there are other factors to consider in making and preparing medicinal herbal preparations, such as size, weight, medical issues, contraindications or reactions with other medications, mental state, physical stability, etc.

Diagnostic Tests

Sometimes tests are helpful. Unfortunately, many of the tests in orthodox medicine either leave toxic residues or even worse. There's a chance you might not live through it.

Why do you think they ask you to sign a release saying you know it could cause a stroke, heart attack or even death?

But if the effects of the tests are so toxic that they are comparable to the disease or even worse, then are they really beneficial?

In other words, if injecting radioactive dye that will never leave your system and is carcinogenic (toxic, cancer causing) is an option, then maybe a wiser choice might be to specify symptoms and find herbs that either diminish the effects or that strengthen the system.

Often these tests are called 'Routine Procedures' implying that there is no danger, but when you look at the statistics, they are not that high in your favor.

Non-Invasive Tests

If there is a non-invasive test that you can have, then, sure, why not? Such as a blood test to see if there's any sign of an infection, or a vitamin test to check your B12 levels or Vitamin D. But what if you didn't have anything that bad wrong with you and you ended up with a stroke, perforated bowel, heart attack or dying? The treatment should not exceed the disease! I'm not sure in what book it says that's ok.

Sometimes a test can be helpful in knowing the direction of your herbal treatment or to know if it's working, such as a blood test for platelet count, white blood cell production, infections, etc. But only if it's not risking the end of your life.

Nothing could be as bad or as uncomfortable as that. Pharmaceutical companies and doctors love to say that the risks of the disease outweigh the side effects of the medication and procedures, but is that really the case when death or stroke is a side effect? What could be worse than that? Doctors take a Hippocratic Oath to do no harm, don't they?

Pharmaceutical Medications

Properly Prescribed

"About 2,460 people per week are estimated to die from drugs that were properly prescribed and that's based on detailed chart reviews of hospitalized patients," says Light, who is a professor of comparative health policy at Rowan University School of Osteopathic Medicine in Stafford, New Jersey. That does not include overdoses or using prescribed drugs unintended, that is PROPERLY PRESCRIBED, meaning you used it as instructed following your doctors' directions.

Leading Cause of Death in US

According to *Death by Medicine*, by Gary Null, Ph.D; Carolyn Dean MD, ND; Martin Feldman, MD; Debora Rasio, MD; and Dorothy Smith, Ph.D the findings from their research concludes: 'The most stunning statistic, however, is that the total number of deaths caused by conventional medicine is an astounding 783,936 per year. It is now evident that the American medical system is the leading cause of death and injury in the US.' That's staggering!

These are mothers, fathers, brothers, sisters, aunts, uncles, grandparents, and children that are dying needlessly at the hands of those who they are trusting to help them to restore health, vitality and well-being.

Instead they're either admitted to the hospital for no reason, put on antibiotics for something that they wouldn't even be used for, encounter a medical error, or die from being prescribed some medication by a doctor.

These are upstanding citizens paying huge premiums for insurance or expensive doctor and hospital bills out of pocket. And they are literally being killed!

Bring In Backup

If we've tried every herb we can and for some reason we are just not seeing any improvement then it might be time to bring in back up, but it's what kind of backup you call in that can be the difference between life and death.

Alternative Practitioners

Seek out a Naturopathic Doctor in your area or a Holistic Health Care Practitioner, Homeopath, Functional Medicine Doctor, Clinical Cannabiniod Clinician, Acupuncturist, etc. Acupuncture is another healing modality that many have never tried.

If you are experiencing discomfort and 'nothing' seems to be helping, this could be due to energetic blockages along your meridians or energy pathways that run through the body. The gentle yet effective pressure from Acupuncture needles can be just the remedy when all else fails. Acupressure is similar, not involving the use of needles.

No Research Showing NyQuil Increasing Recovery Time

When the body produces a fever, it's an effort to kill some kind of pathogen such as bacteria or a virus. If we stop the body from producing these defense mechanisms, we not only are stopping our body from fighting with its natural defenses.

We take Benadryl or Tylenol to lower a fever, which only inhibits the immune system even further with its compounds that the liver has to filter and tries to process on top of fighting an invader or trying to keep them at bay.

Obviously, too high of a fever is very dangerous. But there's lots of research showing that cold medicines do not decrease the length or duration of a cold. There is no research showing that taking NyQuil or any other OTC medications has any effect on increasing the recovery time.

On a molecular level, our bodies can only process that which comes from the natural world. Our bodies were not made to process all of the chemicals, vaccines and medications we inject into it. It has nowhere to go, it sits somewhere, causes inflammation and then disease.

Whatever medication you are on, there is an herb that can do it better! Take back your health, don't just stop taking your prescription by any means, many of them cause more adverse effects if you discontinue use without tapering it off.

If your issue is high blood pressure, there are herbs for that, thyroid dysfunction, there are herbs for that, cancer, there are herbs for that- no matter what kind of disease it is, heart disease, there are herbs for that, diabetes, there are herbs for that, neurological disorders, there are herbs for that, pain, etc.

Take Your Body Back From Big Pharma

Tell them where to go, don't do it yourself, and don't do it all at once. But find a doctor you trust, ask them about natural alternatives to your medications, if they don't know, research it yourself, find a doctor you trust that has dealt with your condition before and feels confident about helping you switch over to a more natural, healthy, immune building way that will keep you out of the hospital, off of oxygen and enable you to have a better quality of life. If you have done your research correctly, they should mention some of the herbs or supplements that you found in your search.

Even though it seems ok, now, at some point your body can take no more, find a better alternative, now, before you get to that point. Just remember, do it safely, under a doctor's advice, if you end up killing yourself you might as well have stayed on their medications. So do it responsibly, do it for yourself and do it now, enjoy the health and vitality that you deserve and that you were put here to enjoy!

Black Box Warning

Are you familiar with the Black Box Warning in your pharmaceutical medication box? Most people don't even read it. There are two lists of side effects for medications, the ones that are life threatening such as stroke, heart attack, kidney failure, liver damage, thyroid dysfunction, hemorrhaging, death and the ones that are not, such as nausea, headache, vomiting, muscle pain, inflammation, shortness of breath, dizziness, etc.

When the list of side effects is larger for the life threatening side effects than the less serious side effects, it has what's known as a 'Black Box Warning.' How can something even be offered to us that can cause such dysfunction within our bodies? How can we even agree to that? Unless Assisted Suicide is a law, I don't know how it could even be legal much less ethical to prescribe a drug to someone with such life threatening dangers.

What could be so bad that it would be worth risking any of those severe side effects? It has become such the norm that people don't even think anything about the side effects, anymore. But they're not even side effects, these are DIRECT effects of the medications, the side effects are any possible BENEFIT you might experience.

Non-Steroidal Anti-Inflammatories (NSAIDS)

As an example, has anyone ever read on a bottle of Tylenol, Ibuprofen, Advil that it could cause a heart attack, stroke, GI bleed? And not after prolonged use, the first time, there's a possibility that this could happen with no warning. GI bleeds happen more often than people think. According to Dr. Sunil Pai, '100,000 people a year go to the hospital from taking NSAIDS, 22,000 people die a year from taking these drugs.

From 1984 to 2009 almost 300,000 people died from taking nonsteroidal anti-inflammatories. That's more people than died in the Revolutionary War, more than the War of 1812, Mexican American War, Spanish American War, World War One, Korean War, Vietnam, Persian Gulf and Iraq and Afghanistan combined.'

Just to give you an idea of how many innocent lives Big Pharma is destroying with their poisons. These are people who just were experiencing pain maybe from a golf injury or twisted the wrong way, picked up their grandchild when they shouldn't have, were shoveling snow, innocent people that trusted that if a product was sold 'over the counter' that it meant that it was safe to take.

And there's now proof that NSAIDS deteriorate your joints. After 2 years, you can see visible changes on x-rays demonstrating that it actually makes arthritis worse.

Aura

Our bodies are more than just what we see in the physical world. Every living cell in our bodies is vibrating at its own frequency. Each cell literally has an electrical current vibrating from it. So in the 60s when the Beach Boys were singing about 'Good Vibrations' and the whole positive vibes movement was exploding, they weren't far off. We are made of energy, consisting of more than one body.

Ancient civilizations have spoken of these other energetic bodies but for those skeptical we now have Kirlian photography which can pick up the subtle bodies and transfer a projection into a photograph. For the purpose of this book we will limit it to our aura.

Our aura is the energetic field outside our physical one. Virtually all healing energy comes through the Astral layer of our aura. It is kind of like a transmitter, picking up subtle energies from our environment and then translating them into the physical body. When we experience blockages, these can also be visible with Kirlian photography.

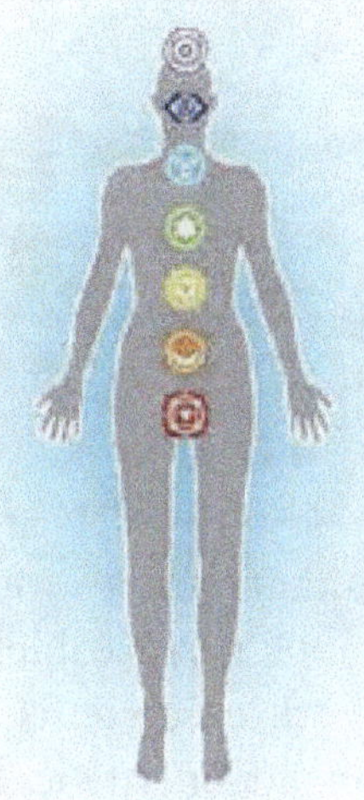

So, when we are full of energy, you can see it illuminating or radiating in various colors around our body. When our energy is low, this is visible as well. So much can be read from an aura photo.

Chakras

When we experience blockages in our energy centers it can cause energy to stagnate. What do we mean by energy centers? We have seven Chakras that we will speak of now for the purpose of this book. These energy centers are found along our spine and are similar to spinning vortexes of energy. They are each correlated with various organs and systems in our body. When they become blocked, we can see a deterioration of energy in those areas corresponding to these energy centers.

The beauty of mushrooms is that they not only affect the physical body, but they also have an obvious, noticeable, recordable effect on the energetic body as well. Some disease stems from a physical imbalance, but much disease begins on an energetic level before it reaches the physical body.

This confirms the importance of stress relieving and Mindfulness Techniques to clear away negative energies or blockages imperative to optimum health. We cannot only address the physical body and expect to affect the whole by ignoring the energetic body.

The body translates emotions into physical chemicals and hormones in the body that are either causing stress sending the body into 'Fight or Flight' or that are reducing cortisol and other stress hormones such as adrenaline. These hormones can be helpful when needed for short term stressful situations but when the body lives in this constant state, it can interfere with neurotransmission of chemicals needed for vital health.

Immune Boosting

Some folks enjoy supreme health, almost taking it for granted, but for some, the idea of optimum immune function seems out of reach. However, if we look further into what 'proper immune function' even means, we might be better able to apply these principles into our everyday life so that it isn't some drastic lifestyle change, or huge purge of everything close to us, but rather a consistent stream of constant choices that steadily lead us on the path to a healthier more resilient immune system.

First of all, where is your immune system, even? Do you know? I bet one guess might be your white blood cells, which is a good one, but there's so much more to it. Your tonsils are part of your immune system sitting as tiny reservoirs of white blood cells attacking any invaders that enter through the mouth before they can reach the internal organs.

That's why when doctors recommend removing them, it's not always necessarily the wisest option and other possibilities or underlying factors should be investigated before the removal. In the 1960s when it became popular to remove children's tonsils, those children had more cavities than the children who still had their tonsils, not having that protection.

Briefly, our thymus gland, under the breastbone, produces T-cells, which are the most active and most daring lymphocytes or fighter white blood cells, there are several types of white blood cells. Helper T-cells identify invaders and stimulate the production of other immune cells located in the spleen and lymph nodes.

Other important areas of lymph tissue throughout the body include the appendix and throughout the intestinal tract. 80% of our immune system lies in our intestinal tract, which explains why having healthy bacteria (probiotics) in the correct concentrations to ensure health and longevity is vital.

Viruses

Dangerous viruses such as HIV have some DNA, although not the complete molecule, so they invade a healthy cell, stealing its DNA and use it to propagate and increase in number. This host cell can be a blood cell or any cell in the body, eventually, this parasitic action results in the cell becoming 'bleached out' by having its nutrients expended causing it to rupture and spew the virus into healthy tissue which it continues to invade. Not only limited to autoimmune diseases or cancer.

Imbalances

Symptoms of poor immune function include:

- **dark circles under the eyes**
- **cravings**
- **sinus problems**
- **joint and muscle dysfunction**
- **headaches**
- **coughing**
- **rashes**
- **emotional behavior problems**
- **mood swings**
- **respiratory problems**
- **food sensitivities**
- **hay fever**

All of the above are signs of an immune system whose function is being diminished by some imbalance that either originates **chemically**, **physically**, or **electromagnetically**.

Improving immune function includes many different facets and is not limited to any one choice, action or medication. So many different factors contribute to immune boosting and optimum immune function such as increasing white blood cells, increasing available energy in the body, removing blockages, removing causes contributing to diminished immune function, improving circulation, detoxing the liver, eliminating factors contributing to increased stress levels, lowering stress levels, lowering cortisol and adrenaline levels, improving digestion, absorption and bioavailability of nutrients, purifying the blood, improving mental clarity, practicing Mindfulness Techniques, gratitude, forgiveness, increasing serotonin and oxytocin or love chemical hormones, strengthening your macrophage, balancing your gut biome, etc.

Chemical Imbalance

This could either be food related or literally chemically related such as toxins you are exposing your body to in the form of personal care products, cleaning agents, air fresheners, chemicals you work with such as at a salon or garage, etc. Something as simple as not getting enough vitamins and nutrients can play an integral role in wellness.

Nutritional deficiencies can cause all kinds of biochemical reactions in the body. A good, organic multivitamin, food derived, might be a wise, healthy choice to optimize immune function and what an easy place to start?

So, if for some reason you didn't eat all of your recommended daily allowances of vitamins and minerals for the day, you know that your body is not lacking in the vital compounds required.

Physical Imbalance

Could stem or originate from some trauma, accident, abuse, blockage, etc. and can usually be corrected by some form of Chiropractic care, not always cracking.

Electromagnetic Imbalances

Includes but not limited to cell phones, Wi-Fi, EMF's (electromagnetic fields) such as emanating from appliances, microwaves, electronics, Smart meters, cell towers, 5G, etc.

Emotions

Emotions are integral to well-being as I stress again and again. If we are continuously angry, unhappy, hurt, stressed, etc. we are continually sending stress messages to every tissue in our bodies, every living cell feels the tension, the pressure is real.

Sometimes, eliminating these factors in our lives seems impossible if our work situation is less than perfect or our coworkers rub us the wrong way. This is why our down time is so important. If your work situation is less than perfect, then it is even more important to de-stress and practice Mindfulness Techniques.

What are Immune Compromising Lifestyle Choices?

Well, to name a few:

- **Diet**
- **Microwaves**
- **Technology**
- **Environment**
- **Personal Care Products**

Some we have control over and can change...some...not so much.

Which is all the more reason to make the necessary changes where you can... because there are some choices we make that are unavoidable, like getting in a car every day, not much choice there if you need to work or take your children to school or go buy groceries.

But, do you have to choose to drink something that will take the paint off of a car is the question? (Referring to Coke)

If we look at each of those very briefly:

Diet: The SAD (Standard American Diet) is actually disease causing, what with the GMOs that are not even allowed in other countries, high fructose corn syrup, sugar, soda, etc.

Follow this link to find out more:

https://www.youtube.com/watch?v=7sUNxX0OxP8

Microwaves: When food is cooked in a microwave, it actually changes the cells within the food into carcinogens...aka cancer causing! How can it be called food if it causes cancer? Food is supposed to nourish the body...sustain life.

Here is a link to review:

https://www.huffpost.com/entry/microwave-cancer_b_684662?guccounter=1&guce_referrer=aHR0cHM6Ly93d3cuZ29vZ2xlLmNvbS8&guce_referrer_sig=AQAAAHn7b7dmC022e5U9pApm1u_0zRsRd1WjvdriVfDFQJbl_09zbgJhRm46Y_1Iw8HJvqu9nGe3Aw7IdXi7MaU13wREJbGF8TIBGk6hHmFQgbKkvMM7v24s3DYQetS5AcSM7UyAvFzTPMi0Mmj4hRtO0ncKR22 UoZljvHq4sWdO-Qs

Technology: The amount of time spent with your device in your hand, on your person or near your head while sleeping is enough to cause cancer. Here is a link to review:

181022_EMF Studies from Powerwatch.pdf

Environment: Depending on where we live, we could be drinking polluted water...chlorinated, fluoridated water, etc. We could be breathing toxic pollution from factories nearby, exhaust, perfumes, bleach, cleaning products, etc. We can be in close proximity to cell phone towers, 5G, power plants, electrical stations, etc.

Skincare Choices: Our skin is our largest organ, absorbing 60% of what we put on it. Most products sold contain toxic, cancer causing chemicals because there are no regulations on body care products in the US at this time.

Even products labeled organic and natural, sold in health food stores and natural food co-ops, can still contain these chemicals. 'Natural' labeling doesn't really mean anything, anymore. See Annex B for more information about toxins.

We see that many of the choices we make in a day can compromise our immune system. If we are not immune compromised, we might not even notice. But if we are, these should be avoided at all costs. Our immune system has to be what cures us, not medication.

When my husband was undergoing treatment, we received the little booklet that goes along with chemo about your blood and what symptoms would indicate what feelings, for instance, low red blood count would mean you would feel sluggish and tired. I realized how when we feel certain symptoms it is because our body is lacking in something.

Which usually always goes back to something that Nature can provide. Do you need to boost your white blood cell count? Lower your blood pressure, increase your energy, increase your appetite? Fight infection? Improve circulation? Support a healthy metabolism? Detoxify? Absorb vital nutrients? Whatever it is, Nature can help.

Free Radicals

Another word for positive ions that you might have heard of before is 'free radicals.' These can either be atoms, molecules or ions with unpaired electrons. 'Stealing' electrons from healthy cells to neutralize their own charge, they weaken healthy cells, causing cellular damage and decreasing the function of our immune systems. In the world we live in today, there are way more devices producing positive ions than in the past, creating electrical imbalances in the air and in our bodies.

Antioxidants fight free radicals which explains why incorporating as many antioxidant rich compounds into your daily routine can help slow down the aging process as well restore many imbalances that nothing else seems to repair.

No Pain Fibers on Internal Organs

As stated, our internal organs do not have pain fibers so they send out signals to other places in our bodies alerting us that there is something wrong. Some health professionals know how to read these signals, some don't. Some know how to mask these signals; some know how to respond to these signals.

Autoimmune Disease

What happens to our immune system when autoimmune disease occurs? And do we need to suppress the immune system to get a handle on the symptoms? Maybe we should remove our immune system like they do with everything else when it doesn't function properly...take it out.

Would you do that with your car? Would you think there was a part in there that the mechanic who built it, put in there for fun, not function? So, when the car starts experiencing difficulties running smoothly, we just take out that part?

For people who believe in God or any other Infinite Creator, do you believe that the Creators in all of their wisdom just had a bad day when they made your thyroid? A bum part? Oh yeah, we have recalls on all of the thyroids, tonsils, uteruses that were made that year, they all had to come out.

No, we were not meant to be sick, we were meant to experience life, vitality and health. Unfortunately, if you are reading this from the United States, then your food supply has been poisoned.

GMOs

How do GMOs and autoimmune disease tie together? GMOs cause inflammation, we know most diseases stem from inflammation. Inflammation causes autoimmune disease as well as many other diseases. If we think about Leaky Gut, or Intestinal Permeability, the gut lining has been damaged to the point of allowing proteins and other bacteria and food particles into our bloodstream, many of these bacteria and proteins mimic the molecules of our own tissues, which is known as molecular mimicry.

When our immune system recognizes these foreign invaders in our blood and goes out to destroy them, the tissues in our joints resemble the molecules in the bacteria. So, our immune system doesn't stop with bacteria and proteins, it tries to be very thorough, recognizing those molecules as similar to the foreign invaders. It starts attacking our joints, which explains rheumatoid arthritis and other chronic joint pain; MS, fibromyalgia, hyperthyroidism, crohn's disease, etc.

Leaky Brain

There is even a syndrome known as Leaky Brain where the Blood/Brain Barrier has actually become damaged and permeated and these large particles of food are actually passing through causing all kinds of brain fog, memory problems, etc. Our immune system ends up getting irritated so much every time we eat, that it gets overstimulated and starts reacting to everything we eat. The answer is not to suppress it; it's to stop irritating it.

Antibiotics

Antibiotics annihilate your intestinal bacteria, which you need. It is recommended that after you've been on antibiotics, you take probiotics with several, specific strains for 2 years.

Why Is Inflammation So Bad?

Anyone who has inflammation can tell you why it's so bad, generally, it hurts, it's uncomfortable and prolonged inflammation can actually even trigger cancer. Inflammation can be caused by a number of factors and can occur in many places all over the body.

Luckily, we have mushroom medicine, all over the world, no matter where we are, the mushrooms growing around us have anti-inflammatory properties. That is the beauty of herbs that I keep speaking of!

This could explain why so many herbs have similar properties because they are needed all over the world. So, if you are not fortunate enough to have a Boswellia tree growing near you to extract Frankincense from, it's okay because you probably have Oregano or Sage or Turmeric, etc.

Health Problems

A few common health problems that are linked back to inflammation range from cancer and heart disease to diabetes and obesity. Our diet is a huge factor, since GMOs have been introduced into the diet, America has just gotten sicker and sicker, we have the best medicine available everyone says, yet we are the sickest country.

GMOs

Causing inflammation, our body doesn't recognize them as food, so there is no way to process it. Our bodies function meticulously, perfectly in infinite harmony with each body system, unless we eat genetically modified organisms, none of the systems in your body know what to do with it. Molecularly, it doesn't match anything in

Nature that our bodies know how to digest.

So, each system is like, 'I'm not taking it, you take it,' and so on, sort of like hot potato, until it ends up just sitting somewhere causing inflammation. This is a vicious cycle that goes on every time you eat, if you are not eating organic food. EVERY time, you know how stressful that gets for your body?

Stress

Can cause inflammation.... Of course, inflammation is caused by other factors, but for the sake of this section, we are sticking to one subject. Inflammation damages your cells and arterial walls and can cause high blood pressure, high cholesterol, joint pain, arthritis, digestive disorders, etc.

Every day the choices we are making are either causing inflammation or reducing inflammation....think about that....especially   if you are trying to cure, prevent or rid your body of disease. So, think about that, the next time you go to eat something, *is this going to cause inflammation or is it going to reduce it?*

Why Natural Health?

Herbal based medicine has been around forever, people have turned to the mushrooms around them for support, nourishment and overall health because that's what was available. There weren't any options for a plethora of pharmaceutical drugs at their disposal with an immense amount of side effects to them, some even including death.

And I even bet that if you communicated with a prehistoric person that there was an option available that could kill them or do unnecessary damage to their internal organs, they would opt out.

Herbal Based Medicine

But there just isn't the awareness necessary for the Herbal Based Medicine Approach to undergo the drastic change that is called for at this time, YET. This is precisely why there are so many Health Rangers out there trying to shake everybody up and show them the truth about the medicines that they are taking, the foods that they are eating, the vaccines they are injecting in their bodies, the personal care products that are being applied to the skin every day and what kinds of chemicals they are using in their homes.

Minimize Recurrence of Disease

If we have a strong immune system which can be built up with herbs, essential oils, Homeopathics, etc. all stemming from Herbal Based Medicine, we will be able to fight most pathogens we are exposed to.

By limiting our exposure to toxic chemicals and compounds in our everyday life, as often as possible, we can ensure healthy immune function. By supporting our bodies with Holistic Health practices that incorporate healing the body, mind and spirit, we can minimize the occurrence or recurrence of disease.

Infinite Intelligence

Many mushrooms have adaptogen properties to them meaning that they find the necessary repairs to make within your body. They just know what you need and target the area where relief is required. Talk about Infinite Intelligence!

Drug Induced Sleep

For folks who take prescription medication to try to get to sleep, many of them don't feel refreshed upon waking because a 'drug induced' sleep does not have the same physiological effect on your body as when your body naturally falls asleep.

Which is why herbal medicine delivers such outstanding results as it is familiar molecules and compounds to the ones your body naturally produces triggering neurotransmitters in your brain to secrete hormones specific to the plant's properties.

Function of Circulatory System

Comprising of a vast network of vessels transporting oxygen and nutrients to the heart and cells while removing waste products.

Function of the Digestive System

Responsible for transmuting food into energy and eliminating waste. Consists as a lengthy, twisty tube that processes food ingested breaking it down into smaller molecules and by absorption transforms it into energy used in various body systems.

Function of the Lymphatic System

Processing toxins and filtering your blood, an active part of your immune system with lymph nodes throughout the body. Comprising of around 600 nodes and vessels removing impurities, maintaining fluid levels by removing excess fluids in tissues, playing a prominent role in fatty acid absorption.

Function of the Reproductive System

Providing multiple functions involved in the reproduction of offspring including sperm and egg cell production, carrying and sustaining these cells, supporting and tending them through development to maturity.

Function of the Respiratory System

Comprising of tissues and organs responsible for proper breathing and the exchange of oxygen and carbon dioxide. Resembling a piping system transporting oxygen into the lungs and cells and providing a release for carbon dioxide as a waste product.

Summary~

In this chapter, we learned the way to treat a patient, we have a basic understanding of imbalance, the causes and effects of lifestyle choices. We know how to stabilize, detoxify and rebuild after an illness.

We understand the Healing Crisis and why it happens, knowing the potential that distilled water has for detoxification and the importance of removing toxic overload so that our immune systems can perform at their optimum level.

Knowing the complexities of herbs and the importance of researching and practicing safety guidelines are now understood. A basis has been laid for the knowledge that because of the cumulative effects of certain herbs, discontinuing use for periods of time during treatment is required.

The beauty of Herbal Medicine has been explored as well as the vital importance our thoughts play at the time of blending including the value of listening to yourself and any possible plants that pop into your head.

We are now clear as to the dangers of diagnostic tests.

We understand the warnings involved with pharmaceutical medications, including NSAIDS and the effects they have on our joints after 2 years.

We know what the leading cause of death is in the US and how to avoid it.

We understand how easy it can be to make ourselves feel better and how easy it is to make the right choices and how what is right is not always popular and how what is popular isn't always right. Grasping the vital importance our emotions have on our health and the connection between what we eat and how we feel is understood.

The connection between GMOs, Leaky Gut and Leaky Brain have been made. Understanding how fiber works in the body and the danger inflammation is to our health and the detrimental effects of drug induced sleep are now clear. We now appreciate the Infinite Intelligence of Mother Nature and value the medicine she has given us.

Chapter 6 ~ Cancer

"There is no chance, no destiny, no fate, that can hinder or control the firm resolve of a determined soul."

—Ella Wheeler Wilcox

In this chapter, we begin to understand how everyone's body has cancer and that if it is growing instead of being caught and destroyed by our immune system that this means there is some kind of breakdown or dysfunction within. What the contributors are to this level of dysfunction will be identified with ideas for how to correct them.

We will understand that we did not get cancer and now we are sick that cancer has specific conditions that are required for it to grow. Understanding these basic principles and how to eliminate the stable breeding ground for pathogens to thrive, we can keep our bodies cancer free.

Comprehending all of the dangers associated with chemo and radiation as they are laid out including their shortcomings. We begin to understand that it only begins with chemo and radiation treatments and that the drugs associated with them are numerous and perpetuate Big Pharma and the endless cycle of 'take this for this and take this for that'…

Some alternative treatments will be investigated as well as herbs that cause apoptosis or cellular suicide of the cancer cells.

Everyone's body has cancer in it, everyone? Yes, everyone's body naturally has cancer cells in it. A healthy immune system that is functioning at its optimal level will find any cancerous cells and destroy them. It is the beauty of the human body in its Infinite Intelligence.

When we make poor choices that hinder our immune system function is when it misses the cancer cells that keep reproducing, going by unnoticed. It is like a miscommunication. Your immune system can do a lot, but it can really only do so much and perform a specific amount of functions at any one given time.

If your toxic overload is too high, then your immune system becomes clogged, bogged down, performing at an inferior level; state it however your brain understands it, but it is challenged. And if you keep challenging it, it will start reacting.

Your body tries to send you signals so that you will stop making these unhealthy decisions, such as heartburn, gas, indigestion, bloating, food sensitivities, chemical sensitivities, joint pain, headaches, difficulty breathing even...but do we listen? No, we reach for the Tums, Tylenol, Advil and any other number of over the counter drugs that I'm not familiar with but you probably are if you frequent Rite Aid or Kinney.

According to Dr. Rashid Buttar, it is estimated that 9 out of 10 cancer patients don't die from the primary cancer, they die of metastasis so it seems like we should be focusing on how to stop the cancer from spreading. Many of conventional medicines tests and treatments can cause metastasis. According to the Epidemiology and Genomics research about 18% of cancers are attributed to infection, making them preventable.
Obesity is responsible for one in five cancer deaths. Which is thought to be a correlation between insulin resistance. The single most effective treatment for addressing insulin resistance is fasting. The majority of cancers are not caused by organic chemical imbalances in the body; they are caused by external factors, environmental and our personal choices. Because someone in your family had cancer definitely

does not necessarily mean that you have to. The same genes that turn on cancer are the same genes that turn it off with micronutrients.

Toxic Overload

If we remove our toxic overload, eliminate the causes, diminish our inflammation and discomfort or dis-ease, then our body can start putting its energy into healing instead of fighting...inflammation, disease and toxins it is exposed to.

Poor Choices

People never want to think that 'they' could be the one causing this disease in their body. If you are wondering what 'poor choices' I could be speaking of, I have listed some of them below.

Food

As mentioned before, if you're food choices are not fresh, healthy, organic, life sustaining foods, then herein lies the problem. GMOs cause inflammation. It is becoming more and more common knowledge that inflammation is the root of all disease. If we can remove the inflammation, by eliminating the components that cause it, then our immune system is freed up to really start fighting whatever diseases have progressed while its function was impaired.

Stop eating out!

If you are sick, stop eating out! Your food needs to be prepared lovingly by someone you know who cares about you and puts healing intention into it. Not to mention you know what goes into it, which is imperative during the healing process. Once in a while maybe, but really limit it to special occasions.

Once you are better, you can go out more often if you have to because your body will be stronger and able to deal with it. If you have cancer, remember, everything you put in your mouth is either feeding your immune system or the cancer.

Eating a 1/4 cup of peaches twice a week lowers a woman's chances of breast cancer by 40%. Bring on the peaches!

Cancer Feeds on Sugar, If You Have Cancer, Avoid Sugar.

Many folks do not know that cancer feeds on sugar or believe me when I tell them. It is true, cancer cells have receptors on them that feed on sugar. Cancer cells consume 15 times more glucose than normal cells. Consuming sugar can speed the development and progression of disease.

So, when you have cancer and you eat sugar, you are literally feeding your cancer. Crazy, isn't it that Oncologist's have a bowl of candy on the counter for you when you come to see them, right? Not many other doctors do that….hmm, probably just another one of those coincidences, huh?

When my husband was undergoing chemo treatments, the nurses would come in the room and ask him if he wanted a milkshake. The refrigerator on the chemo unit was filled with Coke and Sprite and plenty of ice cream. There is a lot of job security in that. Does that mean that Oncologists do not know that cancer cells feed on sugar?

PET Scan

Of course, they do, ever heard of a PET scan? The patient is given a form of radioactive GLUCOSE and then waits for the scan and it is evident where the cancer lies because it is consuming the glucose more rapidly than the normal cells, right? So those groups of cells light up, showing exactly where the cancer is hidden.

Remember I said about invasive tests, during this test with this radioactive dye that they are injecting into you that you sign another waiver for that even says that you shouldn't let a child sit on your lap for a specific duration after, I think it was 24 hours, but don't quote me on it, I got distracted at the part that you are so toxic that a child can't sit on your lap!!

Now that does not mean ALL sugar. After I tell patients this and then recommend they drink 8 oz. of organic fruit smoothies every day, they say, "What about all of the sugar in fruit?"

Fruit Sugar

This is different. Fruit sugar is made by Mother Nature, it is good for you. Refined white sugar isn't. (Read more about this in Chapter 1) Fruits of all foods, being most capable of altering the chemistry of our blood enabling us to better adjust to the seasons and climates where we live.

Artificial Sweeteners

Artificial sweeteners, cane sugar, Sucanat, raw sugar, any of those really aren't good for a compromised immune system. Remember what we learned in the second chapter? Maple syrup is okay as well as honey and Stevia. They actually contain oxalic acid which helps to destroy cancer cells.

According to Cancertutor.com 'refined sugar and other simple sugars also interfere with your immunity system. These substances also interfere with getting vitamin C and oxygen into the cancer cells. Sugar also depletes the body of key minerals and other nutrients because of its acidity.

Acidity

It is not the acidity that directly destroys the minerals, the acidity causes the body to use the minerals to regulate the pH level in the body. The same is true of all acidic foods. The chain reaction caused in the body by acidic foods due to the body's attempts to keep the blood at a level pH — is the cause, or a major contributing factor — to almost all chronic diseases, including cancer. It would take an entire book to describe how the body keeps its pH normal, and the ramifications of these processes.' You can find the rest of this article at:

https://www.cancertutor.com/cancer-diet/

Oxalic Acid

If we think about it, understanding that foods that contain oxalic acid kill cancer cells, then we can relate to the fact that everything we put in our mouth is either feeding the cancer growing inside or shrinking it. Consuming a diet rich in oxalic foods, let's say at least 50% of your diet every day, will be directly destroying cancer cells.

Remove That Which Does Not Serve You Anymore

You need everything that your body comes in contact with to be strengthening it, building it, giving it energy, making you feel good. That includes those around you and where you let your mind dwell. If you are surrounding yourself with toxic people and situations, you can eat all of the oxalic acid you want, but your struggle will still be real.

Healing Process

Part of the healing process is forgiveness, appreciation and removing that which does not serve you anymore. Think of the people in your life. If when you think of someone, you get a pit in your stomach and you start feeling stressed. Avoid contact with them so you can allow yourself to heal. Surround yourself with those who make your body feel alive and happy when you think about spending time with them.

Tannins

Black tea is very high in tannins. In countries where black tea is consumed in large quantities, they see higher rates of esophageal cancer; however, where the black tea is commonly taken with milk, the elevated cancer rate is not seen. Tannins are rendered insoluble by the milk; the protein of the milk being bound to the tannin.

Nutritional Deficiencies

How often when you go to your doctor do they ask you what you've been eating, or if you've been getting enough nutrients? Nutritional deficiencies can cause all kinds of biochemical reactions in the body. By simply taking an organic, food based multi-vitamin we can ensure that our nutritional needs are met and give our bodies what they need to not only just perform their daily functions, but fight any invaders or disease that is lurking. In this easy way, if for some reason, you do not eat 3 nutritious meals, your body is not paying the price. Your body is your friend, it sends you signals, listen to them!

Personal Care Products

Look at the ingredients in whatever you are applying directly to your skin, your skin is your largest organ absorbing 60% of whatever you put on it. If you are applying chemicals to your skin every day, then what result do you think will come about?

And if we think we're untouchable, when you get to be middle aged and you've been applying that makeup or using that face creme or hair dye or hair spray, etc. for 20+ years, the effects can be devastating. I have included a list of the toxins found in skincare products, what part of your body they affect and the derivative. Please see Annex B for more information

Methylparaben/Breast Cancer

Found in over 20 breast tumors when they dissected breast tumors removed from women suffering from breast cancer! When a woman is diagnosed with breast cancer, some Oncologists advise against methylparaben - an ingredient found in many personal care products. But if they knew it was carcinogenic, then why is no one giving women this vital information before they have breast cancer?

You don't have to remove your breasts; women have other choices that they are not informed of by their doctors. Having a mastectomy and continuing to use cancer causing products is not going to stop you from getting cancer, it will just stop you from getting cancer in your breasts, that's all. The chemo that is used for fighting breast cancer is known to cause cancer. It's true, ask your Oncologist. Read further…

Tamoxifen

It is a little known fact that the chemo used, Tamoxifen, to treat breast cancer in the medical field is a known carcinogen. Why do they treat cancer with something that causes cancer? And they know this because they won't say you're cured until you're five years out because they know it's likely to recur.

As we stated earlier and cannot stress enough, a cancer patient needs to be loved, cared for, nourished, strengthened. If you have breast cancer, know someone who does or are just trying to educate yourself, Dr. Véronique Desaulniers healed her breast cancer naturally and is an amazing woman, doctor and resource, look her up!

Electromagnetic Smog

Many imbalances in the body can actually stem from interference from outside influences and invisible waves that are being emitted by appliances, Wi-Fi routers, cell towers, etc. Don't even get me started on microwaves! We are all electrical beings; every living cell in our body is vibrating at its own frequency.

If we carry our cell phone in our pocket, put it up to our ear...The World Health Organization has confirmed that cell phones cause cancer, it is no mystery. My grandson was actually taught in 4th grade not to sleep with a cell phone within 4 ft. of your head!

This is vitally important information... how many teenagers and adults that you know sleep with their cell phone if not on their bed, then definitely within 4 ft. of their head?

Structural

Go see a good friend recommended Chiropractor. I have heard amazing stories resulting after Chiropractic care. Blockages can result when our body systems are not functioning as they should. Removing these blockages can result in blood flow and energy releasing and dispersing, stimulating the body's 'Vital Force' to heal itself. This does not always include cracking, some is light, gentle and exceptionally effective, such as Biogeometric Integration and are worth looking into.

Emotions

It is a fact that our emotions, our mind, what we think can literally make us sick, every time. Even if we eat right, exercise, take vitamins, if we are mad, guilty, resentful, hurt, these emotions can play a key role in you getting sick and where the sickness will show itself. Forgive and be grateful, no one is worth your health, go talk to someone if you have to in order to feel better about a traumatic memory.

Every experience we have attaches an emotion to it and when we think of that experience, our bodies feel what it was like to be there at the moment. On a cellular level, you are right back there, so only think of things that make you feel happy. Our perceptions change our cells, so keep it light and keep it positive so that your body can focus on regenerating, not reducing cortisol levels.

Stress hormones shut off your immune system, which is why when they perform organ transplants they give the transplant patient stress hormones to stop their immune system from functioning and rejecting the new organ. Try to keep them at a minimum.

Discover the Essence of Plant Medicine

Turn to Nature, if you believe in God/Creator then you believe he made all of the herbs, if you believe in the Universe than you know that these herbs are here to heal us, whatever your background, race, religion, if you trace back to your roots, your ancestors had certain herbal allies that they turned to in times of distress that cured whatever symptom they were seeking relief from.

There is always an herb for whatever ails you it's just a matter of finding the right one. Many of the conventional treatments either by causing cancer or by breaking down your immune system are so dangerous that they are literally worse than the disease.

When we found out that the chemo they gave my husband for his Lymphoma caused cancer and asked if it was true, his Oncologist confirmed it.

But they didn't inform of us of that before they gave it to him, which he felt was almost underhanded and he felt a little tricked. Doctors take a Hippocratic Oath to 'do no harm.' There has to be a better way to treat cancer than with cancer causing agents.

Will To Live!

There are so many different ways to stimulate your immune system, no matter where you live. Be diligent, educate yourself, never give up hope! When they asked my husband if he had a Living Will, he said, "No, I have a Will to Live!"

Chemo and Radiation

When my husband was in the hospital awaiting his chemo to arrive and to be mixed, I spent the night in the bed next to him and when the nurse came in in the morning she told me, 'Once he starts his chemo, you will not be able to touch him anymore.' (Another nurse told me when I asked her how long it was that I couldn't touch him anymore for, that she would never tell anyone that and that cancer patients need hugs, kisses and close contact, I chose to listen to her.)

When he was undergoing his 5 day long in-patient IV chemo treatment and would urinate into a handheld urinal from his bed, the nurses would put on suits and gloves just to empty his urine into the toilet. That's how toxic his urine was, *but it's OK for it to be inside of his body,* I wondered?

Blood Transfusions

Did I even mention the need for blood transfusions? So, as if it's not enough that you have cancer, no, now we can try introducing a blood borne disease onto that! That'll be another waiver you're going to have to sign! They never told my husband when he signed up for chemo that he might have to have blood transfusions.

No mention of that AT ALL, if that is a typical procedure that goes along with your treatment, shouldn't you be told of it ahead of time? Once he had the chemo IV in his arm they said, "Yes, next week, your blood levels will be so low that you will have to have a blood transfusion." They told him that he'd have to have one after every treatment - that would be four - he didn't even want one!!

In the end, we did really well, the plants I was giving him would bring his numbers back up before they would say he had to have a blood transfusion and the nurses could never believe throughout his treatment when we told them that he had not needed one blood transfusion.

He only had to have one, near the very end and they didn't even ask, or anything, they just brought in a bag and started hooking him up to it and when I asked what was in it they said, "Oh, he needs a blood transfusion, his numbers are low."

We looked at each other, we were so upset, we felt totally violated, if anyone had told me, I would've upped the herbs or something, but we were never privy to that information until it was too late. And no one even asked, first?!

Stem Cells

Previously, it was thought that any cell in the body could become cancerous when its DNA was damaged. Now we know that cancer cells are actually stem cells. Stem cells sit quietly just waiting to see what kind of cell they will be. We have them all throughout our body and they haven't decided what they're going to be yet.

They could turn into a lung cell, they could turn into a brain cell, a liver cell, etc. They are very primitive cells. Damaging the DNA of stem cells causes them to become immortal. It wakes up the cell. So, it starts reproducing at a rapid rate, which becomes a cancer. The mother stem cell is what creates these daughter cancer cells.

Mother Stem Cells

Chemo and radiation are effective at merely destroying the daughter cancer cells, which create the tumors. But it is the mother stem cells that are creating those daughter cells. That's why after those two treatments, they will say they got it all because the tumor went away, but that's why they don't say you are cured, they call it 'Remission,' because they know it's likely to come back.

Chemo and radiation actually strengthen the mother stem cells and that's why the cancers usually come back more aggressively than they were in the very beginning. The only way to kill the mother stem cells is your immune system. If your immune system kills it, odds are it will not come back.

More Aggressive

After chemo and radiation, it comes back infinitely more aggressive because of the micro environment of the stem cells. Because of the production of a lot of cytokines or inflammatory chemicals around the stem cell which is caused by chemo and radiation, causing greater DNA damage, resulting in more cancer that is more malignant than it was when it started.

In 6 months later or less, it's going to grow a lot faster and is more likely to metastasize and mutate becoming more resilient to other treatments and causing secondary cancers, resulting in an enrichment of the actual mother stem cells and enriching the population of the tumorigenic cells, at the same moment. And resulting in secondary adverse effects from these treatments such as neuropathy, damage to the heart valve, lung damage, loss of teeth, ulcers, 'chemo brain,' digestive disorders, etc. these treatments perpetuate the need for pharmaceuticals.

Perpetuates Big Pharma

So, because chemo causes nausea, they give you a pill for that, then you cannot eliminate properly because of the constipation it causes, so you need two pills for that; a laxative and a stool softener. Then it's necessary to make sure that you're urinating enough so they give you Lasix. Because chemo destroys your friendly gut bacteria, ulcers and other digestive disorders are a result, so they prescribe you a pharmaceutical or two for that, chemo causes dry mouth and sores, so then they prescribe you something for that.

Their killing off your blood cells in your bone marrow, and you literally will die if they're not replaced. So then you need to get a $20,000 Neulasta shot in your bone which is also very painful and can cause bone pain for up to a week after the shot, so then if you need something for the pain, they've got you there, too!

If we talk about lymphoma, that would mean there's cancer in the lymph nodes, right? Our lymph nodes are what filter toxins out of our body, our lymph system is part of our immune system, removing impurities and working as a filter removing toxins and pathogens.

So, if your lymph nodes were swollen so much to the point that you were in pain from the swelling, then adding numerous chemicals into that already toxic overload could not only push the body too far causing the balance to tip completely but would just compound the damage and increase the swelling. And that's exactly what it did.

Now, let's just think about that for a minute, we'll take my husband's case as an example. Before he got into treatment, he had swollen lymph nodes on his esophagus, trachea and abdomen. By the time it was at its worst and he could no longer lie down because the pain was so severe, the lymph node on his neck under his jugular vein was the size of a golf ball, no joke, I am not exaggerating. Talk about scary.

Ray's Story

Instead of jumping around here and there, I will just begin at the beginning of my husband's story to give you a complete and full understanding of what I am speaking of. My husband is a General Contractor, Plumber, Electrician, Roofer, etc. In April 2016, he did a rather large roofing job all by himself, which translated into him carrying numerous bundles of heavy shingles up and down a ladder and many hours of bending and squatting on the roof completing the job. By the end of the job, he had extreme back pain and attributed it to the roofing job.

My husband is a man who works until dark, I have to force him to take weekends off, he is so motivated, driven to get the job done. When he would leave in the morning and I'd ask him what time he was coming home, he'd say, "When the job is done." And I would always tell him that some people stop working at 5 o'clock, you know? But not him he is a devoted, hard-working individual. Always putting others first, not even stopping for lunch, barely drinking anything all day long and if he did it was coffee.

If I asked if he drank any water that day, he would always say, "Yeah I had three or four coffees." To which I would reply, "That doesn't count for water, you know?" And he would always reply, "Well it's made with water." In other words, he was always in a constant state of dehydration, not that either one of us were really aware of it.

But in hindsight now we know. In order to neutralize one cup of coffee, one would have to drink 35 cups of water which he definitely wasn't doing so his system was all out of balance. Although he did only eat organic food, it was pretty much only at night when he came home from work.

The intensity of the pain grew, then it became hard for him to swallow, anything I would try to give him, he couldn't take. He would always say that he felt full or that he couldn't get it down his throat; that it would just stop in his throat. I was juicing for him and making him smoothies and herbal teas which he would insist that he couldn't get down.

So, as the pain got worse and worse, he started coming home earlier from work, started missing work, which was unheard of for him! He started lying down in the daytime which I've never seen him do in the 20+ years I've been with him and complaining all the time about his back and the severe pain he was in.

Again, completely out of character for him, this is a man who never complains, or ever acknowledges his pain, his body would hurt all the time but he'd just work through it, like so many laborers do. But if he wasn't working and was complaining about the pain we all knew it must be really bad! Our worry grew. My daughter, Marijah, brought over a bottle of CBD Oil which we had never tried before, at this point. So he started taking that.

Knowing that we didn't want to go the conventional route but knowing that I needed backup, I started looking for a good Chiropractor in May. We found a good one in Hardwick, but unfortunately, it didn't help much, Chiropractic care was not what he needed at this time.

At this time, we did not have a Primary Care Provider, because we never went to the doctor, there was no need for one. He hadn't been to a doctor in probably 30 years, at least 20+ that I had known him, he was always healthy. As soon as he started displaying such severe symptoms,

I began trying to find a Primary Care Provider for him, but because we were new patients, the wait list was so long, we were waiting for an appointment for a new patient visit after filling out the packets.

I hadn't been going to farmers' markets once he started not feeling well because I was afraid to leave his side. At that time, I attended more than one farmers' market a week and I was also a Market Manager for a farmers' market that I had started in our town. I had new vendors coming on this particular day, so I had to go.

My daughters were at the house with him, so I felt OK to leave, knowing that they would take good care of him. For lunch that day I made him some soup and he only ate like two spoonsful of it. A little while passed, I went down to the market, helped the other vendors find their places, set up my booth and went back to check on him.

When I got back, he was even worse than before I left.

I didn't want to leave and go back down to the Market. I asked if he had eaten anything and he said, "Yes," the girls had made him food. Seeing him like this, I asked if someone could pack up my booth and let the other vendors know that I wouldn't be returning. I went in the kitchen to try to make him some more tea and I noticed the same bowl of soup that I had tried to get him to eat hours earlier sitting there. And there was no other food prepared in the kitchen.

I went back to where he was and asked him if the girls had made him food and he said, "Yes, I ate soup." But then I told him that that was the soup that I had given him earlier and that it remained untouched. They had tried to make him food but he refused. It's hard to eat when you are in so much pain. So, he hadn't eaten anything all day.

As a firm believer that food is medicine, I NEEDED him to eat! Food would give his body the strength it needed for this fight. The pain was taking over. He was getting weaker and sicker by the day.

You lose time, when you're going through something like that. The fear is crippling. The helplessness is terrifying. I started doing the math and realized we were at the two month mark. The pain grew more and more intense to the point he was crying and began vomiting, I asked him, "Do you think that it could be something else? If it was your back it would've gotten better by now, it's been two months, do you know that?"

Sometimes he's not a real good judge of time and I didn't know if he realized how much time had passed. Days were slipping by and he was caught in the unclenching grips of unbearable pain, losing sleep, disoriented. I begged him to go to the emergency room, insisting that if it had been just from the roofing job the pain would be gone by now and this wasn't the first time, he just kept refusing.

After he threw up the first time, he came out of the bathroom and showed me that his lymph node right by his clavicle on the left side of his neck, his supraclavicular lymph node, was huge. I noticed that it was corresponding with your stomach. And I said to him, "Don't you think that's kind of ironic that the lymph node that corresponds with your stomach is so swollen and you're throwing up? Let's go to the hospital." He didn't want to go but he was desperate once he started throwing up because of the pain. So, we went.

We don't like taking any kind of pain medications because they make us nauseous. But at this point the pain was so bad he was vomiting, so nausea would be the least of his worries. We went to the hospital and the doctor looked at him and said, "Oh you're dehydrated." We tried to tell them how bad his pain was but they didn't pay attention and hooked him up to an IV.

By this time his pain had kind of subsided so when they asked him how bad it was, he didn't lie and say it was off the charts, he told the truth, which to them didn't seem alarming. So they asked him, *Do you want some pharmaceuticals?"* He said, "No. He wanted to know what was wrong with him."

So after the IV drip was over the doctor came back in and said, "Oh you look so much better," and looked at me and said, "See he looks all better, doesn't he?" Gesturing at his lymph node, I asked, 'What about the swollen lymph node on his neck? I've never heard of dehydration causing swollen lymph nodes."

And she looked at him and said, "Oh you're getting a cold?" And he said, "No I'm not." And she said, "Oh you're getting over a cold?" And he said, "No I'm not." And she said, "Well, just keep an eye on that," and left the room. We headed back home thoroughly discouraged. He didn't want to go in the first place, "That was dumb," he said on the way home. "They didn't even do anything."

We came home and he started soaking the sheets at night, sweating profusely, the pain started up, after a few days, the pain got so bad again that I begged him to go back to the emergency room. "They're not going to do anything," he'd say. We went back to the hospital again and they asked him if he wanted some pain medication and didn't really care.

We tried to tell them that the pain was so bad that he would just stand there for hours leaning against the wall and crying out. But they would ask him what his pain levels were and he would tell them the truth, which wasn't that bad at the moment, so they would just ask; "Do you want some pain medication?"

But he didn't, he just wanted to know what was wrong with him. He wanted to get back to work, the pressure of knowing he was not completing the jobs that he was in the middle of working on when he got sick was literally eating him up inside.

So, he started taking the pain medication. But it wouldn't really work, the pain was still there. It would knock him out, allowing him to sleep, but he was so knocked out that he couldn't even function when he took it. He wanted to get back to work more than ever. He took it with the hope that if it killed the pain, he could at least function and get back to work, but that's not how it worked.

He started getting really mean. Not acting like himself at all, which I think was a combination of the disease, the pain and the pharmaceuticals. When he wasn't sleeping, or being grumpy, he'd tell me things he was going to do because he wasn't in as much pain. But that 'Ray' was only in for a very short window of time.

That was the 'Ray' that was not in pain, but hadn't felt the effects of the narcotics, yet, so he was clear and pain free. Unfortunately, this only lasted for about 15 minutes before the narcotics would kick in and he'd have to go lay down unable to do any of the things he just said he wanted to accomplish.

One day he said he wanted to go for a walk, he hadn't been outside at all besides to go to the hospital and spring is a beautiful time of year in Vermont, the warmth we waited all winter for was finally here and he hadn't enjoyed it at all. Just sleeping all day, every day. I was SO excited he said he wanted to go outside and a tiny part of my heart thought maybe the old him was back. But then the pain pill kicked in and he said he was going to go lay down and I was like, "It's beautiful outside, do you want to still go for that walk?" But his answer was, "No, I'm just gonna go lay down."

It was awful to see him like that, and I began to wonder if this is what our life was going to be like? With him on narcotics, sleeping all day, when he wasn't grumping about something until either pain set back in or he was knocked out. It would be a lie if I said I didn't cry more than once at the idea that this was our new life. He started being like, "Where's my pain pills?!"

Like a different man, which I understood because of the situation he was in, but it didn't make it any easier to watch. I kept wondering if I would ever see my old Ray again? Not that I blamed him, because I was glad that he was able to at least sleep with the pain pills so that he was able to get a break from the pain but all the time knowing the damage that they were doing to his lymph nodes because your lymph system is the one responsible for filtering toxins.

Which brings us back to the very beginning of how this story began. So, if his lymph nodes were already being taxed, then taking a bunch of pharmaceuticals, narcotics especially, was not going to help his body, at all.

I began noticing the lymph node getting bigger and bigger when he started taking the pharmaceutical medications. He started noticing that he couldn't go to the bathroom anymore. This being an issue for him, made him not want to keep taking the pharmaceuticals. He started eating prunes, basically drinking flaxseed oil, drinking quarts of prune juice at a time. But nothing was really doing it.

Mad at the pharmaceuticals, he stopped taking them. Once he stopped taking them and after he went to the bathroom, I could literally see the lymph node on his neck go down.

The pain got so bad again within a few days, he started taking the pain medication, which was doing nothing really, and he kept vomiting from the pain. We went back to the ER for the 3rd time. This visit we had a different doctor who paid attention and said she wanted to take a CAT scan.

The scan results showed swollen lymph nodes on his esophagus, trachea and abdomen. They told him that they would set up an appointment for him to see an Oncologist and that they were thinking cancer. I, of course, was astonished that they would go right to cancer. "What else could cause swollen lymph nodes," I asked.

And they said an infection but that they were really steering towards cancer and that he needed to get a biopsy done. They gave him a stronger prescription until he could get in and the hospital assigned us a Primary Care Provider in Hardwick and I had an appointment for one in Plainfield the following week.

I instantly ordered some Turmeric tincture and Red Clover flowers, B17 and Essiac Tea after the CAT scan results, once I knew what I was dealing with. I started giving them to him, the tincture 3 times a day, tried to get him to drink the Essiac 3 times a day and giving him the B17. These are major cancer killers and while I didn't even want to go there, that perhaps that was what was plaguing my husband, but just in case, I knew these were powerful allies to have on our side.

A friend of mine referred me to an amazing Kinesiologist in Montpelier and we went to see him. When we got there, he said, "You know they're thinking cancer, right?" He put a bunch of supplements in his pocket and tested my husband. My husband indicated that his body wanted the Turkey Tail Mushroom. "That's a potent cancer fighter, you know, and your body wants it." So, he started taking that, too.

I had to show up at the Waitsfield Farmers' Market once in a while to keep my spot. One of these times, I asked an Herbalist what she could recommend after telling her the situation and she gave me an herbal tea blend she had prepared for the lymph system and I started making him take that every day with Calendula and some other herbs.

At this point, I should probably give you a little family history, his mom died of lung cancer, one of his brothers died of brain cancer, one of his sisters died of breast cancer. One of his other sisters got diagnosed with breast cancer right after his diagnosis, (and in the fall of 2020, had a 7lb tumor removed) and little did we know but in January of 2019, his oldest sister, from Missouri, would get diagnosed with lung cancer (and sadly, she lost her battle right after the completion of this book in May 2020.)

If I said he wasn't expecting this day to come, I would be lying. With a family history like that, how could you not wonder if you were next? But I kept telling him even if he had cancer, it didn't mean he had to die.

Herbs take time, though, the pain got so bad again that he was vomiting and gave himself a hernia you could visibly see sticking out on his side. The new pain pills still weren't working and I said, "Let's go to the emergency room at Dartmouth and maybe they will actually do something!" (We had been going to St. Johnsbury.)

My husband was so mad at me for making him go to the emergency room all of these times, he didn't want to go in the first place and then to be treated like there wasn't something really wrong with him when we all knew there was, was just as discouraging. Not to mention, it made him so nauseous riding in the car, every bump exasperated the pain. But I felt so helpless watching him deteriorate like this. What else could I do?

So, we headed to Dartmouth which is about an hour and a half away, once they looked and saw that he had gotten the CAT scan in St. Johnsbury and that we were waiting for the biopsy, they told us that there was really nothing that we could do but wait. I tried to tell them that after he took the pharmaceuticals that I could see the lump on his neck literally get bigger and they would say that's not from the pharmaceuticals and look at me as if I was so naive, thinking that's from the cancer but I literally saw it get bigger and smaller right before my eyes.

'Until the biopsy,' they told us, 'There's really nothing that we could do but wait.' We asked them if they could recommend a good Primary Care Provider at Dartmouth and told them that we needed to get into see someone right away. So, they made an appointment for the following week.

We went from having no Primary Care Provider to three appoint- ments. The appointment with the Hardwick doctor was the first one, so I told my husband, "We will just go and meet all of them until you find one that you like and feel comfortable with." When we were in Hardwick, we met Christine and connected with her immediately.

Her manner was kind, she was gentle, she listened and we had a long story to tell, she never made us feel rushed, she made us feel as if she understood and cared. Probably another reason why I loved her so much was because she was a midwife for years that had turned to Family Practice and was also an Herbalist!

When we left the appointment, I said to my husband, "So the next two appointments are this week and next week," and he said, "I don't want to meet any other doctors I want her to be my doctor." So, then it was settled, we knew we loved her and we knew he wanted her.

In the meantime, my husband started taking Oxycodone, they weren't working so we started giving him one and a half, because there was nothing else to do, the pain was so bad. But it didn't help at all. So, we called Christine and she upped the dose of what he was taking. That didn't help so then she prescribed Hydromorphone. He tried that for a while with not much relief.

Because it was night time, I called the hospital and I told them that he was in so much pain that I didn't know what to do and asked if it was OK to give him more of the pain medication that she had prescribed him. They ended up calling Christine and prescribing him Fentanyl.

Prince had just died not long before that from Fentanyl, so we were very apprehensive about having him use that, especially because we didn't really use any of that and Fentanyl was like, heavy duty! So, I called Christine and said to her that I was concerned about him taking the pain medication because there was a reason he was in so much pain.

And I was concerned that maybe he had twisted an organ or something, or an infection or something that if he couldn't feel the pain, he could end up hurting himself and damaging whatever was out of balance even further. She said to me, "Michele if they are thinking that it is cancer, then the best and only thing that we can do for him is to minimize his pain until he can get into see the surgeon and the Oncologist and get the biopsy.

You don't have to worry about it being a twisted organ, that is not what we are thinking it is. Although the results are not conclusive, yet." She told me, "It's up to you, if you can just keep it at bay with the herbs, until he's able to get in to see the Oncologist and surgeon, you can buy us some time."

I was able to help him, but if he couldn't take what I was trying in earnest to give him, and the pharmaceuticals were exasperating it, but they were the only thing that allowed him to sleep after not sleeping for weeks, I didn't know how we were going to get him back and I couldn't believe that his whole life was hanging on a thread and that is was dependent on me! I had dealt with numerous childhood maladies with success and felt confident in dealing with children's issues, but cancer…a life threatening disease…and it was all up to me!

But no pressure, though. I had faith in the herbs and myself implicitly, but he couldn't take them and was continuing with the pharmaceuticals, I feared how long this cycle could go on until it would reach complete disaster.

Hopeless, I hung up the phone and we got the Fentanyl patch. It was a last resort, we had tried the other medications that she had prescribed for him, the Hydromorphone, he was taking as much as he could and it just wasn't cutting it.

My daughter, Marijah, was over and in her worry for him, she earnestly convinced him to try the patch and put it on him. After she left, we read the side effects, one of the warnings said to beware that his temperature didn't spike or he could die…he had been soaking three sheets a night! His temperature was definitely spiking. When he heard that, he immediately ripped it off and just continued with Hydromorphone.

We went to the emergency room the fifth time because he was vomiting and that lymph node on his neck was so huge it was just scaring me! His jugular vein looked huge and the lymph node was the size of a golf ball from all of the pharmaceuticals and the cancer. He was sweating profusely and moaning in agony. I called Christine and she said that if it got that bad to go to the hospital and to tell them that our doctor said to come and to ask for steroids. I had given him the pain pills before we left, he didn't even want to leave and he was throwing up, I had to pull over on the way to the hospital so he could throw up he felt so bad, cursing me out the whole time!

We walked in and it ended up being the same doctor as the original visit when she had told him that he was dehydrated, my heart sank. We went in and I said to her, "Do you remember us?" I said it kind of confrontationally, because I was mad at her. I did have deep feelings about her and the way she had treated us and I did wonder if she had taken it more seriously in the beginning if it would not have progressed to this point.

He was almost dead. And she said, "What?" and I said, "Remember we came in and his lymph node was swollen and huge and you said he was dehydrated? And we told you he was in so much pain and you sent him home and did nothing? Turns out it was something! And they think he has cancer! He has swollen lymph nodes on his esophagus, trachea and abdomen they gave him a CAT scan, look at his neck," and I gestured at his neck. And Ray, being his mean, impatient self on narcotics was like, "Just tell her what Christine said!"

My husband has a very hairy chest with hairs coming out from the top of his T-shirt. And she reached over to pull his T-shirt out so she could see the lymph node better and pulled some of his hairs. He said "Ow!" and looked at her, and she didn't say she was sorry or anything she barely looked at him and said, "I'm trying to see your lymph node!" And I could see he was getting madder.

And I said, "We talked to our doctor and she said that if the pain got so bad to come to the emergency room and to ask for steroids and that the steroids would take down the swelling." The doctor looked at me and said, "Oh she did, did she?" With a very mocking tone and patronizing look on her face.

"Let's go!!!" My husband hopped down and walked out. As we headed out of the parking lot, I had to pull over for him to throw up, swearing at me the whole time. "Let's go to Dartmouth," I said. "No, take me home! I'm not driving to Dartmouth right now!"

Unable to go to the bathroom again, trying everything even store bought laxatives, he quit taking the narcotics again, determined to go to the bathroom. After a few days of diligence with the prune juice, laxatives and Flaxseed oil, he had success. Again, I saw the lymph node on his neck decrease in size.

In the beginning it was hard for him to take the herbs I was trying to give him, the tincture made it a little easier because I could squirt some in a small bit of water and it was just one quick sip he had to swallow. The night sweats had subsided now, and we were two weeks out that he had been taking the herbs, Essiac Tea, Turkey Tail and B17 since the results of the CAT scan and it was the morning of the appointment with the surgeon to get the biopsy.

And we woke up together, since he had started enduring the extreme pain, he would go back and forth from one bedroom to the other... pacing... leaning on walls. But this night, he stayed in bed with me all night. I looked at him and said, "Look at you, you look so good!" He was lying in bed with me, woke up happy, he was smiling. "I wish we didn't have to go for that biopsy. This is the best you've been in months!" And it really was, since April.

Now we were into the first week of June. I even wrote to his sisters and told them how much better he was doing. But our four daughters were freaking out and wanted answers and were scared to death. So, we went for the biopsy.

When we were talking to the surgeon, we told him the journey that we had had with the five emergency room visits and asked him if he had ever seen anyone go from soaking 3 sheets a night and being in so much pain that they were throwing up, to now, not being in any pain? And he looked at my husband and said, "Well you're on pain pills, right?' "No, I'm not on any pain pills. I'm on Turkey Tail Mushroom," he said.

The surgeon had never heard of it and we told him all about it. He was very interested in it and asked me to send him info and then took what he called a gun and proceeded to take five chunks out of that swollen lymph node on my husband's neck.

The pain came back with a vengeance! After that biopsy, I couldn't get him back. We had another week to wait for the Oncologist appointment and he was in agony, again. Standing around all night, writhing in pain on the bed. I would go lie down and get up and ask him if he needed anything and he would go from bedroom to bedroom trying to find a comfortable position.

With no luck, he'd get up and I would try to follow him but sometimes I would fall asleep in one of the bedrooms until I realized that he had moved and then I'd get up and go in the other room to be with him.

At my wits end about how to help him, watching him suffer, knowing there's nothing they'd do because now we were waiting for the results from the biopsy. I remember one day watching him sitting in the chair just sweating profusely, eating or drinking was not even an option in this condition, just moaning because he was in so much pain.

Having given him his pain pill, so I couldn't give him anymore for hours, feeling like he was dying before my eyes. I got a pan and just started soaking his feet and added essential oils to the water, I didn't know what else to do. I would try to force fluid on him, but he would keep saying that he couldn't swallow.

So, I got up one morning after falling asleep on accident and he was sitting in the chair. And I said, "How long have you been sitting there?" He said, "I sat here most of the night, I can't lie down anymore, it hurts too much." I said, "What?! I'm calling that Oncologist's office, this is ridiculous!!" "It's ok, he said, I can just sleep sitting up." "No, that's not a thing, people don't sleep sitting up." I called the Oncologist's office and left a message because they weren't open yet, informing them how we weren't scheduled for an appointment for another week.

I told them how he couldn't even lay down anymore. The secretary called back and said, "If he's that symptomatic, get him in here, right away." But I had just given him his pain pills and he was like, "Not going anywhere, I just took my pain pills." "Okay, we'll go in 4 hours when they wear off," I told him, so frustrated that I finally got the appointment and he wouldn't leave!!

When we finally got to the ER, they did some tests, they checked his heart, kept asking if he had any chest pain. "No, I keep telling you I don't," he'd say. By the time we got to the hospital, the pain was not as bad, as always happened when we went to the hospital for some reason. Two doctors came in the room with very serious looks on their face and explained that clearly by the looks of him he appeared to be OK, but that according to their equipment, he was having a heart attack.

And that they were going to bring in the Cardiologist. Nurses and aids began bringing in equipment and running like crazy around the room seeming very concerned. And I said to my husband, "I think they're pretty worried about you," and he just laughed and said, "Yeah, it looks like it." The cardiologist kind of came running into our room and when he saw my husband stopped in his tracks, kind of laughed and said, "You don't look like you're having a heart attack." My husband said, "I don't feel like I'm having a heart attack!" The Cardiologist brought the EKG over and said, "Let's take a closer look."

Turned out that my husband had Pericarditis, which is fluid around your heart, because the lymph nodes in his esophagus, trachea and abdomen were so swollen, they were putting pressure on his other organs which were squeezing his heart.

In an effort to protect his heart, his body put a protective sack of fluid around it so that it had the space that it needed without being pressured. Which is great, the only problem is that you can't live with Pericarditis for very long. So, in other words if we did not get him in when we did, he might not be here today.

After securing that situation, we met with the team of Oncologists and did some more tests. They took a sample from his bone marrow from his hip that was so painful that they gave him a medication that causes Amnesia after so that you don't remember the pain. The test concluded that he had Diffuse Large B Cell Non-Hodgkin's Lymphoma but we needed to do further testing. The results of the further tests showed that he had a Triple Hit of Non-Hodgkin's Lymphoma, which means there is the Myc gene present meaning that the cancer cells are very aggressive, growing rapidly and then they found the BCL2 gene present which means that his cancer cells don't die.

With this grim prognosis, they told him that we would begin five day long IV chemo treatments in patient. And that he would need to get six rounds of this. That with this treatment, he only had a 35% chance of surviving and to get his affairs in order. They said when that chemo didn't work, we would continue with clinical trials. After that meeting, they gave me a long creepy hug and told me how sorry they were. Which was very thoughtful and nice but just completely creeped me out because I was thinking, my husband's not dying, I don't need a long hug.

Before they told us what made it a Triple Hit and just told us the prognosis not what those two genes meant essentially, I asked them but didn't really seem like they wanted to tell me, I begged in earnest if they would just tell me, "What does it mean, what do those genes do, if you can just tell me, I can find a plant to deal with it. I just need to know what they do." The Oncologists looked at me sadly as if it was pathetic to see me think that I was going to be able to save my husband's life with some plants and explained what the Myc and BCL2 genes meant.

After they left the room, we were left with the huge dry erase board in front of us with the words Triple Hit Non-Hodgkin's Lymphoma written on there and Myc gene-very aggressive and BCL2 gene cancer cells don't die and the 35% prognosis. I went over to the board and erased everything they wrote. In big letters I wrote, every living cell in my body is filled with health and light! I grow stronger every day! And I said, "Don't listen to them, we are going to kick this cancer's ass!!!"

In the meantime, they had given him steroids which had taken down the swelling completely and he felt 100% better. They told him it would take a couple of days to get the chemo together and that he would be staying in the hospital while he waited. With Father's Day the next day, he told them he did not want to stay in the hospital, that he would come back, that he felt fine, not to worry, he'd return when the chemo arrived.

They literally would not let him leave, telling him that he could die and that they might not be able to get him in so quick, that he'd have to go through admissions again, that they might not have a room available, all of these excuses which literally almost made him cry because he didn't want to stay there anymore. He actually felt good unlike he had felt in a long time. So, we stayed and he got his first chemo treatment.

As soon as I got the word of what exactly we were dealing with, I immediately started researching any spare moment I got. I stayed by his side the whole time, preparing him organic food and making sure he was comfortable. It was only when he slept that I was able to diligently research. There were a few herbs that I knew of besides the ones he was taking and I asked his Oncologist if I could start administering them to him, too. The Oncologist said that most were ok, but that he couldn't take the Turkey Tail Mushroom because of the possibility of bacteria or contamination. I called his Primary Care Provider, 'Christine' and confirmed that it was fine for him to take the Turkey Tail Mushrooms because they were in capsules, it wasn't like a raw mushroom out of the woods. So, he continued taking that as well.

I did have to stop juicing though, because after chemo, his immune system was so low, if there was a microscopic piece of dirt on a carrot it could literally kill him. So, I chose not to take the chance, knowing that I had alot of other avenues for getting those nutrients into him without risking his life.

When we got the confirmation that it was cancer, I ordered CoQ10 for him because cancer cannot live in an oxygenated body. I also ordered cell food for him which he drank three times a day in his glass of water or juice that oxygenates your blood. I brought the blender to the hospital and would make him smoothies every day. They got me a refrigerator in our room because I was taking up so much space in their refrigerator.

They needed room in the refrigerator for Coke and Sprite and chocolate milk. Knowing that cancer feeds on sugar and seeing all of the sugar in the refrigerator on the Oncology unit filled me with despair, how could any of these people heal when the hospital was breaking down their immune system and then they were drinking sugary drinks that would feed the cancer?

I could not believe that these people had cancer and while they were getting chemo they were drinking Coca-Cola! The nurses would come in and ask my husband if he wanted a shake while we were there. Because of the miserable situation we were in and the joy a chocolate shake could bring, I went to the store and bought organic milk and organic ice cream so that if he wanted a shake, he could have one and it wasn't toxic, at least.

They started the chemo and warned him of the headaches, nausea, neuropathy, blurred vision, etc. plethora of side effects that he might experience and that if it got too bad, they would stop the chemo. That this was kind of a preliminary run to see how his body dealt with it. My husband said that he told his body that it was OK to let the chemo in and let it do its work and that it wasn't going to make him sick.

With the supplementation I gave him and his positive attitude, he did not experience many of the side effects of chemo except hair loss. He was able to go to the bathroom on his own, he didn't have any headaches, he didn't experience any pain, he wasn't on any pain medication, the nurses would come in and ask him what his pain levels were and couldn't believe that he wasn't taking any pain medication like everyone else on the floor.

They couldn't believe that he didn't need anything from them, that he felt good. When they would walk in the room and ask him how he was feeling, he'd say, "I feel great!" They would always tell him what an easy patient he was.

I had brought our Buddha statue from home and had a salt lamp in there as well as some crystals and always had his favorite music playing, when they came in they would always mention how nice his room was and how different it felt. And even though he didn't need anything, they would stay and talk to us for long periods of time and tell us how much they enjoyed our talks. All of his nurses were angels and made his stay there the best it could be.

While all of the nurses were nice, I did have to keep my eye on them giving him unnecessary medication. They would come in and say it's time for whatever pill they wanted to give him and I would say, "What is that for?" And they would tell us and I would say, "Does he have to take that?" And probably seven times out of ten they would say something like, "No you don't have to take it, we just always give it to everyone on the floor." I would then explain that he had Lymphoma and so we needed to minimize his chemical intake. And that he was already taking so many chemicals that we couldn't stop so we needed to eliminate the ones that we could.

During all of this, one of the times he was in the hospital, one of his friends from CT came visiting, he has a Practice in RI. He told us that the woman he shared his office with was a Kinesiologist but trained in Advanced Nutrition Therapy and that there actually was another one like her in Newport. He gave us her number and said to just check it out and if we liked her, awesome, if not, forget it.

We went and saw her and fell in love right away, she was so kind and sincere. I loved her methods. So, we brought in all of the supplements that my husband was taking and she muscle tested him and told us how many of each his body preferred. She also recommended some other supplements. Throughout his healing journey, we would routinely go back and have him tested and the amount of supplementation he needed changed over time. It was invaluable having that kind of insight throughout the healing process, to achieve that confirmation and know that we were on the right track.

Later on, after his treatment, when visiting with Christine and discussing our journey with her, she confirmed that his lymph nodes definitely could've been getting bigger or smaller depending on the amount of toxins in his system. I wasn't sure why the hospital felt the need to play it down and minimize me and tell me that it had nothing to do with the medication when I could clearly see that after he took it the lump got bigger and then smaller when he didn't. If it was the cancer growing it wouldn't have gotten smaller.

After the first round of chemo, they checked his blood levels and said that they were going to up the chemo 20%. Then after the second round of chemo, they said that they were going to up it 20% again because his numbers were still so high when they checked his blood. I couldn't help wondering if it was me, with all of the supplements I was giving him that was keeping his numbers up.

When I asked Christine, she said it was definitely what I was giving him and to keep it up. She said it was incredible how far they could knock him down and how quickly I could bring his numbers back up. That's not to say that the week after chemo he didn't feel like he was dying. The week after chemo, all he did was mostly sleep, was super weak, and needed to regain his strength for his next round.

He had the chemo every three weeks. The week after was when the effects of the chemo made him feel so weak and then the two weeks after were for him to feel strong again so that they could knock him back down. We did this for three rounds with him doing great not feeling any of the side effects besides the loss of energy.

Medicine Buddha~

Ray and I had been together over 20 years, but we weren't married when he got diagnosed. He asked me to marry him after his diagnosis. I guess he figured 20 years in, it was a safe move. Because of our daughters and college schedules, we had to rearrange the date for the wedding many times. We'd pick one date and it wouldn't work out, so we'd randomly pick another that sounded good and check with each girl. My husband wanted a very private ceremony with just the girls and a couple close friends.

One of the only dates that would work with the girls was August 18. When I was inviting one of our close friends and explaining how many times we changed the date and gave her the chosen date. Her eyes lit up and she said, 'That's Medicine Buddha Day!

She showed me a picture of him. While I love Buddha, I am not Buddhist, I have read his teachings and haven't found one that did not resonate with me as with many other religions. So I am not partial to one, but love elements of them all. However, my friend is Buddhist, she started explaining a little more about him to me.

She said, 'He was the first doctor, he's the one who brought medicine to the world. He took 12 vows to heal mankind. Hearing his Mantra is healing, reading his vows is healing, seeing his image is healing. 'He's going to be healed,' she said, 'what are the chances you'd pick that day??''

She actually had sung a Medicine Buddha Chant that was on YouTube that we listened to many times over the next few months. I started studying Medicine Buddha and thinking of ways we could honor him in our wedding. We also put up images of him so that my husband would see him in the car, at home, the hospital, etc.

Like I said, I never wanted to leave his side. He would always tell me that I should go to the market while he was in the hospital getting chemo because the nurses were there to care for him. So, one of the days that I felt ok to leave his side, I was driving to the Waitsfield Farmers' Market while he was getting his chemo treatment, I prayed to Medicine Buddha and I asked him if he would help me heal my husband? I asked him, 'if you will help me heal him, I will get an image of you tattooed on my right forearm so that every time I give him his supplements, he sees your image…'Faith is a strong remedy. And you have to have faith in your treatment.

The Truth About Cancer

Like I said, I never wanted to leave his side, so I hadn't gone to the farmers' market since he had started the chemo. He would always tell me that I should go while he was in the hospital getting chemo because the nurses were there to care for him. So, I went to the Waitsfield Farmers' Market one day and a woman asked me if I had face creme. I told her I couldn't make face creme at this time and explained that my husband was sick. She asked if I minded her asking what was wrong with him and I told her.

I said, "But he's getting chemo now, so he's not as bad off as he was." As soon as I said, "Chemo," she looked shocked and gasped and put her hand up to her mouth. "Have you seen, *The Truth About Cancer?*" she asked. "No, I haven't," I said. "You should watch it! It's free on YouTube," she said. "You should really watch it." 'Ok, I will," I told her.

I didn't watch anything around my husband that wasn't a comedy. Everything in his environment was upbeat and positive. I made sure that everything in his experience was kept very light, with no drama or turmoil. If one of my daughters called and had a dilemma, I'd tell them to call their sisters, sorry, so, I didn't want to watch it around him. During his treatments we stayed in a cabin on Lake Memphramagog. One day, I left him there and went to the laundromat and watched it. I knew from that moment on that I didn't want him to ever get any more chemo.

He was scheduled for a PET scan in four days, now we were in September. And I felt confident that he was cancer free, because of all the supplements I had been giving him and I could just see by looking at him how well he was feeling compared to before when cancer was running rampant through his body. I didn't know how to approach him watching it, because I didn't want him to think that he just gave himself cancer and to go into his PET scan thinking that.

People would come by and visit and were always asking about treatment and plans and he would tell them about the upcoming PET scan. And they would ask if he was supposed to get any more chemo and he would say that he was not sure yet. I started saying, "No, no more chemo. You're good you don't need any more of that, I just know it."

I felt as if I had been keeping a secret from him, the night before the PET scan, I told him about *The Truth About Cancer*. I told him to just watch it until the end and to know that he was so bad off that we really had to do the chemo because he couldn't get the herbs down. And in some instances, chemo is necessary and that his case was one of them. And that because of the addition of all the supplements and herbs his body would heal itself and the cancer would not return. All along I kept trying to explain to him how cancer only can thrive under specific conditions and if you make your body inhospitable to cancer, it cannot grow.

I would always tell him, "Remember you started my Herbal Education with that Homeopathy class 20 years ago and it has led us up to this point, so that I can save your life!" I kept trying to tell him that each of the herbs, mushrooms, enzymes, vitamins had their own success rate curing cancer individually. People have cured cancer with just Essiac Tea, people have cured cancer with B-17, people have cured cancer with Turkey Tail Mushroom.

Let's just say that each of them only has a 35% cure rate, which each of them combined, you have a much higher cure rate, but let's just say that each only had a 35% chance and you are on 20 of them?? Your chances are way over 100%!! There is no way you will not be cured! We are making your body inhospitable to the cancer cells; they literally cannot live under such circumstances.

Cancer Free!

Before seeing it, he was still not sure how he felt about quitting the chemo. After he watched it, he was sure too. We went the next day for the PET scan. After, we went into the Oncologist's office to get the results. She said, "Sit down, I have the results but I need to call down there, not sure if they're correct." And we're like what? So she calls down and says, "Hi, I'm calling about a PET scan for Raymond Pike, it says negative, can you tell me what negative means?"

We all looked at each other and I was thinking, *'Pretty sure negative means no cancer.'* "Can you check the birthdate on that for me?" she asked. She even had them check the spelling of his name, she could not believe it!

We were hooting and hollering in the office as we had one of Ray's friends with us that was visiting from California and our Oncologist tried to chill us out from our outburst of joy and said, "Now, we just need to make sure that it doesn't come back. You still have two more rounds." I'm thinkin' '*Not.*' Then she looked in her book and said, "Oh, that's strange you're not scheduled for the two more rounds." And I was thinking, '*Yup, precisely, because he's not going to do any more chemo.*'

Then she checked his blood levels and said that he would have to get a blood transfusion before they could start the chemo again for the fifth round because his levels were so low. All the while I am thinking, so you're going to put five days of the strongest chemo that is intended for some of the fastest growing cancers, into a body that has no cancer, for five days!

So right now, he is a healthy body with nothing wrong with it. And we're going to give him a blood transfusion, risk a blood borne disease so that we can give him five days of chemo when his body doesn't have any cancer?? If that could not cause cancer, I don't know what could!

At this point, I was beginning to feel concerned, I was glad that we were stopping the chemo, not only had he not wanted any blood transfusions, since the very beginning, but I had always been able to bring his numbers up, after, remember? But not now, for some reason. Was the damage they were doing on such a large scale that what I was doing would need to be increased 10 fold to keep up? What if I couldn't get him back? People died from chemo all of the time, while we did great for those 4 rounds, I feared to see what would have happened had we done those 2 more rounds.

No More Chemo

But we didn't say anything in her office; we just scheduled the next round for two weeks. At the end of the two weeks, I called and told them that he had a cold. If you are not healthy, then you can't get chemo. They don't want anyone sick risking infecting someone else who has no immune system. We didn't tell our daughters, because we figured they would want him to do what the doctor said.

Before the PET scan, sometimes the subject of death would come up and I wouldn't have it. I would not talk about 'what if Dad, dies??' That was not happening, so we didn't need to talk about it. Not a conversation I was having. To say that this upset my daughters would be putting it mildly, not having seen *The Truth About Cancer* or having done any research on it.

Stalking Us

The hospital kept calling our house and leaving messages as well as on my cell phone. It took me a few days to call them back and tell them that he had a cold. I left a message on their voicemail one day, after hours, because I dreaded talking to anyone. But they just kept calling.

My daughters knew that he wasn't sick, only one of them lived with us at the time and she heard the message and called her sisters. As far as we were concerned, it was his choice how he chose to manage his healthcare. With the hospital calling the house and leaving numerous messages that if he didn't come in and get his chemo he was going to die, scared our daughters and resulted in a bombardment of phone calls.

The message that I left saying he would not be there for his chemo, they clearly did not get or pretended they didn't or were not taking no for an answer. They just kept calling, it was kind of like creepy, like stalking almost. He didn't have cancer anymore, what was their problem?? His body had no cancer in it, he was just like any other healthy body.

Because I was trying to keep everything in his environment up beat and happy, I tried not to answer their phone calls. Once our daughters knew about it that was the end of it. They made him promise he'd go back and see the doctor. So he promised he'd go back and TALK to the Oncologist.

Final Oncologist Appointment

We made the appointment to tell her we would not be doing any more chemo. When we told her, she of course pleaded with us, ensuring us of the return of the cancer. My husband said, "From what I understand chemotherapy can cause cancer, is that true?" "Yes, we have seen that." "Well nobody ever told me that," was my husband's answer. "I already had cancer, why would you give me something that could cause more of it?" "We don't see it very often," she said. "But you do see it," he said. "Yes," she said. "I really wish that you had told me that before you gave it to me," was his response. And he asked if she had anything to offer him that was not cancer causing??

Hyperbaric Chamber

Then he said to me, "Tell her about the hyperbaric chamber." I told her how cancer cannot live in an oxygenated body. I told her there was such a thing as a hyperbaric chamber that fills your body with oxygen. "Yes, I know we have one in the basement." "You have one in the basement?!" I said. "Why didn't you ever put my husband in there if you knew that it would kill his cancer?" She replied, "It is only used for radiation patients. And it is very expensive." I said to her, "And chemo isn't?"

And she just looked away and said nothing. We continued talking for a little bit longer and she said, "I can see that I am not going to be able to talk you into it." She said, "Keep up the good research and keep doing whatever you are doing because it is clearly working!"

We started going back every 3 months, now because we're 3+ years out we only have to go back every 6 months. Really, he could just go back annually, but we love his Oncologist and she said she loves seeing us, so we keep it to 6 months (just so she can keep an eye on it.) Every time we go back, she says, "I think you're cured! The kind of cancer you had was so aggressive that if it was going to come back, it would have by now, I think between what we did and what you're doing, you're cured! Keep it up!"

Wildflower ImmunoTherapy

Knowing that your immune system has to be what kills the cancer now is why we are hearing of Immunotherapy from the conventional medicine field. Only there's isn't the same as mine, utilizing compounds that are familiar to the body that actually reduce inflammatory chemicals and stress hormones, that help the brain to produce the correct formation of neurotransmitters so the body receives and recognizes the brains messages while restoring balance on many levels supporting the bodies function instead of either inhibiting it or prohibiting it.

Doctor Who Discovered Radiation Died of Cancer

'The doctor who won a Nobel prize for discovering the use of radiation for cancer treatment, died from cancer from the radiation as well as many other MDs who developed leukemia from testing it on their own arms to find the correct dose,' according to the American Cancer Society's article Evolution of Cancer Treatments: Radiation 6/12/14.

Have a Connection with Your Provider

A few years back, we were in the process of looking for a new doctor because Christine left family practice. We ended up with this doctor who actually tapped her fingers while my husband was talking. Yup! And while he was releasing alot of emotion about how the thought of death always lingers at the back of your mind once they tell you that you are going to die and that their cure for you only has a 35% chance and that you only have a 35% chance of living 5 years out, she actually responded with, "No one's getting out of here alive." Okay, if that's all your doctor can come up with, how compassionate can you expect them to be?

While my husband unloaded a flood of emotion, she kept opening her mouth trying to interrupt him and seriously, rolled her eyes at her defeated effort to interrupt him. She kept darting her eyes and lifting her eyebrows, I mean it was so offensive, disrespectful, downright rude!! She actually said, "We have no idea why good people get disease."

She told him he has no control over his disease, that it has nothing to do with the choices he's made in his life and that coffee has gotten the slip of acceptance, now, that they are finding out that coffee drinkers live longer, when he told her how he stopped drinking coffee because he learned how much it dehydrates you, "Ha ha," she laughed, "that has nothing to do with it!"

How could someone in the medical profession be so naive? 'We don't know why good people get disease?!' We know all kinds of reasons why people get cancer and a whole myriad of disease, alot of them relating back to GMOs and the inflammation they cause in your system.

Not to mention if you are rubbing toxic chemicals on your skin, which is your largest organ, absorbing 60% of whatever you apply to it. How about EMFs (electromagnetic fields) and cell phones linked to brain cancer? Is she kidding? How is she supposed to give you any helpful advice if she doesn't even have a clue where disease begins?

This is what people are left with, if this is what your doctor is like, find another one! Find one that can tell you how to sustain and nourish your body, one who looks at what might have caused your disease or discomfort, one who knows about Epigenetics, and if you can't find one in the conventional medical system, find one that will work with your conventional doctor.

They are out there. If you choose conventional therapies, herbs can ameliorate many of the symptoms they cause. They are working for you, empower yourself, step up, don't be afraid of their white coat, speak for yourself. This is the beginning of your healing journey and it begins with you being your own best advocate.

Cancer Fighters

Cancer is a miscommunication between the body and the immune system. As we've said, everyone's body has cancer cells. Everybody. Because cancer is fast growing rogue, immortal cells, they are rapidly multiplying. By activating the immune system, it will find those rogue cells and destroy them.

The difference between herbal medicine and pharmaceuticals when it comes to fighting cancer is that first of all, the immune system is compromised which as we said led to the growth of the cancer.

Second of all, the body is in a diseased state, so it needs nourishment, care and rest. Pharmaceuticals tax the body's immune system as well as the liver and kidneys. Foreign molecules that are synthetic and produced in a lab can never compare with natural compounds that the body not only knows how to utilize but actually produce biochemical changes in the body which trigger healing instead of masking symptoms, this being pharmaceutical medicines whole premise.

Apoptosis

When we speak of cancer fighters or killers there is a distinct difference. A cancer fighter, in my book, is an herb that strengthens your immune system enabling it to seek out and destroy cancer cells.

Cancer killers are herbs that induce what is called apoptosis. Apoptosis is cellular suicide, in other words, when the cancer cells come into contact with the specific compounds, found only in certain plants and mushrooms, the cells actually kill themselves, commit cellular suicide or apoptosis.

If you are a cancer patient and everything you eat, apply to your skin, or inhale is inducing apoptosis, as opposed to inflammation, your chances are much greater of conquering it. Various choices we make from the moment we wake in the morning to the moment our heads hit the pillow are all adding up to wellness and disease prevention or they are slowly accumulating in our system a little at a time with each unhealthy choice that you think might not be noticeable, but in the long run it always is. Food can be the most potent medicine or it can be the slowest form of poison.

Vitamin C

As with many other nutrients, vitamin C is a potent remedy in the fight against cancer. I would strongly recommend adding this supplement to your *Cancer Free Protocol* to boost your immune system. The thing with vitamin C is you know when you're taking too much if you start having diarrhea.

Then you just back off until you don't and you know that that's a safe level of vitamin C for you. Vitamin C increases immune function in more ways than we will mention in the scope of this book. But the vitamin C that my husband and I take every day is a vitamin C complex made by New Chapter from whole fermented foods so that it is more readily absorbed by the body. There is no point in taking vitamins if they are low budget vitamins.

Perfect Environment for Pathogens

Everything you put in your mouth is either causing inflammation or decreasing it, as I keep repeating. We now know that inflammation is the root of all disease. This translates into reduce your inflammation, reduce your disease. When your body becomes inflamed and remains in that constant state, deteriorating your cells, reducing your available energy because your body is fighting the inflammation, this form of heat that collects in these areas is a perfect environment for pathogens to grow, these are the optimum conditions for disease.

It isn't that we get cancer and become sick.

You were sick and compromised in the very beginning or you would have not gotten cancer. If the body was healthy, the cancer could not grow. The fact that there is a cancer growing indicates a breakdown of the immune system. Only the immune system can kill the mother stem cells that create cancer. And if the immune system is the one who rids the body of cancer, then there should be no more recurrence if the precursors of the cancer are removed.

The people that you see in their 80s with a quality of life similar to what they enjoyed when they were younger lived an active lifestyle, some pharma free or on limited pharmaceutical medications, eating healthy, even using non-toxic household cleansers and personal care products.

Get Medical Advice

None of the information contained herein is meant to substitute for medical advice, if you think you have cancer, go to the doctor, whether they're versed in Western or Eastern medicine and at least find out what it is so that you know what you are dealing with.

Whichever you feel more comfortable with but go see a professional to help you on your journey. Watch *The Truth About Cancer* it's free on YouTube, before you make any decisions, though, if you have cancer, it could save your life!

Not a Death Sentence

Cancer is not a death sentence; your body will heal itself given what it needs, every time! Your body created it, so your body can heal it.

Summary~

In this chapter, we learned how cancer is a form of a breakdown of the immune system, we familiarized ourselves with what inhibits immune function and a lot about what to avoid, such as white sugar, processed foods and GMOs, so that our immune system does not get bogged down or overloaded with toxins from poor choices we make

Ranging from food to electromagnetic smog, even the products we rub on our skin and use every day.

We learned about the toxins in skincare products and how methylparaben, a known cancer causing agent is in everything and is known to deposit in innocent unsuspecting women's breast tissue causing breast cancer and then the treatment used for it is Tamoxifen which is another known cancer causing agent.

We know of the toxicity of chemo and radiation and that it is only something that is recommended as a last resort because of your improbability of surviving. The way that Big Pharma is perpetuated within that cycle is understood.

And we know now what cancer cells are and that they are actually stem cells and that it is the mother stem cells that cause the daughter cells that create the tumors and that chemo and radiation do not kill the mother stem cells only the daughter cells.

An awareness has been raised as to the probability of secondary cancers forming after chemo and radiation that are more virulent than the original cancer. A deeper understanding of the resounding side effects have been explored.

We learned how herbs can save your life instead of end your life. We understand what apoptosis is and the difference between a cancer fighter and a cancer killer. Now we know that cancer cannot live in an oxygenated body and how a hyperbaric chamber can increase the likelihood of us beating the cancer and how we can add CoQ10 to our *Cancer Free Protocol.*

Whether it's an Eastern or Western Healthcare Provider, we know that cancer is something that we should not try to address ourselves and that it's ok to bring in some back up and get some non-invasive tests done to get a better look. And above all, we learned that cancer is not a death sentence.

Chapter 7 ~ Mushroom Profiles

Chaga, Turkey Tail and Reishi Mushrooms we foraged!

"Nature loves courage. You make the commitment and nature will respond to that commitment by removing impossible obstacles."

—*Brian Jackson*

Introduction to Mushroom Profiles

The way mushrooms work in the body, the course their actions take, is so infinitely seamless that only Divinity could have created such a complex yet simple healing system. The differences between the phytochemicals and flavonoids, polysaccharides, omega 3s, essential fatty acids, terpenes that each mushroom holds is similar to its own little prescription specially formulated in Mother Nature's Pharmacy.

Containing specific amounts of each molecule in the perfect formula for relieving so many numbers of symptoms, conditions and ailments that the possible combinations are endless and countless. This is why you should never give up when trying to treat any disease or symptom, once you find the perfect calculations of each specific compound in their adequate quantities developed correctly to your individual specification; then complete healing will resound.

In this chapter, we will explore 3 different mushroom profiles understanding their uses and applications.

How to Use the Mushroom Profiles

When studying the mushroom, notice its curative properties and what conditions it treats and then decide which route of administration you choose. Remember that herbs have a primary function and a secondary function, utilize the primary function for targeting the worst of the symptoms then utilize the secondary functions in a complementary fashion with other herbs that share those actions.

Each mushroom has its own phytochemical constituents, so if it seems like you're not achieving the desired results within three days or immediately in some cases, mix it up, change the dose, bring in some other allies.

Herbs are recognized like old friends in the body, celebrating their reunion, visiting places they haven't been in a long time, replacing vital compounds, clearing out others, like mini house keepers, waking up the good guys and kicking the bad guys to the curb, in no uncertain terms.

To include every constituent found in each mushroom and its properties is beyond the scope of this book, so I will limit it to descriptions of a few of the active constituents.

If we think of mushrooms as beautiful as they are, like soldiers in our army of natural killers and fighters. They each have their own branches of the military (or of your body) that they target, immune function, respiratory, circulatory, nervous system, sometimes we can go with the milder guys, other times we bring out the Green Berets to divide and conquer.

There's a mushroom for whatever you seek, whether you're looking for a strong reaction or a mild one, the choice is yours.

And the beauty of it, you don't have to spend too much time experimenting because we've done it for you, I have given you recipes and included three mushrooms that have been proven through time to restore balance without suicidal thoughts, brain bleeding, liver failure, thyroid dysfunction, kidney damage, swelling of the face and hands, difficulty breathing, irregular heartbeat, shortness of breath, actually they do the exact opposite, they target all of those symptoms with no side effects.

Mushrooms, controlling the course of an illness can give your body the time needed to restore balance. Come with me on a journey discovering the essence of Mushroom Medicine…

Chaga

"Why take medicinal mushroom or herb number one-hundred or thousand when you can have number one? And that number one is chaga."

—*David Wolfe*

Chaga - *Inonotus Obliquus, Hua Jie Kong Jun* (Chinese)

****SUPERFOOD****

Other names: Black Gold, Mushroom of Immortality, Birch Conk, Clinker Polypore, Tinder Fungus, Tree Cancer

Genus: parasitic fungus, wood-decaying mushroom,

Hymenochaetaceae family

Native to Northern parts of the US, Siberia, Alaska, Northern Canada

Name Origin: Russian word for mushroom

Notes:

Siberians referred to it as the Gift of God.

Listed in The Shen Nong Ben Cao Jing, the first century BCE, one of the oldest, most treasured Herbal handbooks of all time.

Known to be one of very few, rare substances on the planet to nourish all of the three treasures: Qi, Shen, and Jing.

Used by the Mesopotamians, Egyptians and Chinese 4000 years ago.

Europe, Asia and Russia have records of using it for medicine as well as indigenous people.

One of the highest sources of antioxidants. (See 'More Information' below)

Contains over 215 different vitamins, minerals and bioactive compounds.

Grows on Birch, Chestnut, Beech, Alder, Chestnut, Hornbeam trees.

Has been known as tree cancer, but it's really a symbiotic relationship according to Christopher Hobbs, 4th generation Herbalist. He maintains that it is part of the tree and an attempt at healing the wound as it is known to grow where the tree has been injured.

Decreased infective properties of the hepatitis C virus by 100-fold in just 10 minutes in some studies.

"Laboratory and animal studies show that chaga can inhibit cancer progression,' according to the Memorial Sloan Cancer Center.

In one of the studies, chaga mushroom extract was given to tumor bearing mice who experienced a 60 percent reduction in tumor size, while mice with cancers that had metastasized had a 25 percent decrease in their number of nodules compared to the control group.

Drying mushrooms in the Sun increases their vitamin D content.

Parts used: whole mushroom

Curative Properties: adaptogen, allergy alleviator, antiallergic, antibacterial, anticancer, anticoagulant, antidiabetic, antifungal, antihyperglycemic, antihypertensive, anti-inflammatory, antimetastatic, antimicrobial, antineoplastic, antioxidants, antitumor, antiviral, appetite suppressant, caffeine free, expectorant, hepatic, hepatoprotective, hypotensive, immune modulating, immuno- modulator, immuneo-stimulant, kidney tonic, neuroregenerative, pectoral, restorative

Energy and flavors: warm, sweet, slightly bitter

Cautions:

1. Check with your Healthcare Provider before use if pregnant, nursing.

2. Check with your Healthcare Provider if you have autoimmune disease as it boosts immune function.

3. Check with your Healthcare Provider if you have blood sugar issues. Chaga alters blood sugar levels so can make it a challenge for diabetes sufferers to regulate blood sugar levels.

Conditions: Alzheimer's, cancer, constipation, Crohn's disease, diabetes, fatigue, foggy brain, gastritis, gastrointestinal cancer, heart disease, hepatitis, hepatitis C virus, HIV, IBS, inflammation, liver disease, malaria, parasites, psoriasis, red, itchy skin conditions, stomach pain, stress, tuberculosis, ulcerative colitis, ulcers

Bio chemical constituents: amino acids, antimony, antioxidants, barium, B-complex vitamins, beta glucans, betulin, betulinic acid, bismuth, boron, calcium, cesium, chromium, copper, ergosterols, fiber, gallic acid, inotodiol, iron, magnesium, manganese, melanin, oxalates, phosphorus, polysaccharides, potassium, rubidium, selenium, silicon, sterols, sulfur, triterpenes, triterpenoids, vanillin, vitamin D, zinc

Parts of the body: digestive tract, heart, kidneys, liver, spleen, stomach

Preparations~

****Because some of the active compounds that are present are not soluble in water such as the terpenes and sterols, a double extraction process is required with mushrooms. First an alcohol extraction, then a decoction to release any compounds not released into the alcohol extraction, such as the polysaccharides, beta glucans and proteoglycans.**

While Chaga can be made into tea, many of the potent benefits are lost without an alcohol extraction. The double extraction method described would be first choice for medicinal property extraction from Chaga. **

Double Extraction Method

Alcohol Tincture:

For mushrooms, alcohol is the preferred medium over glycerin…

Fill jar half way with dried mushroom

Cover with organic grain alcohol

Cap, label, shake everyday infusing with healing intention, love and gratitude.

After 1 month strain.

Decoction:

Place alcohol soaked mushrooms in a pot, cover with twice the amount of water.

1 part chopped up mushroom.

2 parts hot water using triple the amount of water used for the tincture.

Simmer on low heat for 2 to 6 hours.

Water will reduce quite a bit, add more as needed

Cool, compost mushrooms

Add equal parts decoction to equal parts alcohol tincture giving you a 25% alcohol extract if the alcohol was 100 proof (50% alcohol, 50% water).

Cap, shake well, label.

Standard Dose:

½ teaspoon two to three times a day.

Chaga Tea:

Chunks of Chaga equaling around 1 tsp. if not powdered

Soak in cold water for between 1 to 3 hours

Pour just boiled water over chunks

Don't let water boil as it can destroy vital compounds

Let sit for 1 to 2 hours

<u>More Information</u>: Have you ever heard of the ORAC Value? This is short for "oxygen radical absorbent capacity." Basically, it's like this- the ORAC value of Chaga is 146,700. The higher the ORAC value, the better a food's ability to protect the body from disease which causes free radicals.

Birch trees produce betulin in their bark, when this is extracted from the bark, it cannot be used safely, but it has potent anti-cancer properties and is used in cancer treatments. Chaga absorbs and synthesizes the betulin, rendering it safe for human consumption and use. Talk about Infinite Intelligence!

It seems unfathomable to me that a mushroom could increase physical endurance, wouldn't you think you'd have to exercise or something for that? But it's true, Chaga actually can!

One study published in 2015 found that when mice were given Chaga mushroom polysaccharides, the mice were able to swim longer, the glycogen (fuel) content of both muscles and liver increased, while lactic acid levels in the bloodstream decreased.

In a study of mice that was published in 2015 in which mice were given Chaga mushroom polysaccharides, they were able to swim longer as the fuel (glycogen) content of both muscles and liver increased, while lactic acid levels in the bloodstream decreased.

About the photo at the beginning of this mushroom profile, my husband came home from work one day and I said to him, we need to go for a walk. Up behind our house there's miles of forest. 'There's a mushroom calling me…' I told him. I've never felt like there was a mushroom calling me before so it's not like this was a normal occurrence.

But he has met me before so he wasn't surprised. He doesn't question my spirituality and even goes along with it, being very intuitive himself. So, we got the dogs and headed out back. As we walked, I looked around and didn't feel anything. We just walked and talked, hanging out.

Then I saw it! Just sitting there, we've been through those woods so many times and walked past that spot, not sure how we could've missed it. But we didn't miss it this time! When we got back, I called my daughter and grandson to show them the huge Chaga we found and my grandson took one look at it and said, 'Ok, that's a Buddha!

Granted, I do have Buddha statues all over my house, so it's not surprising that his brain might go there, but how cute? After that, I haven't used it for it medicinal purposes, it is reserved for spiritual practices only.

I'm always able to spot Chaga in the forest because there's nothing else in Nature that's that black in the forest except a bear. And it's easy to tell the difference between a bear and Chaga, right? I see it all of the time but I don't take it just it because I see it.

It takes Chaga years to grow, and it is way overharvested. So please just be mindful.

Reishi Mushroom

"Mushroom of Immortality," "King Of Herbal Medicines," "Useful for enhancing vital energy, increasing thinking faculty and preventing forgetfulness." "…refresh the body and mind, delay aging and enable one to live long. It stabilizes one's mental condition."

—Shen Nong Ben Jing Ancient Chinese Text

Reishi - *Ganoderma lucidum, Ling Zhi*

SUPERFOOD

Other names: Ling Chih, Lingzhi (Ling Zhi), "Spirit Plant,"

Ganopoly

Genus: polypore fungus "bracket fungus," belonging to the Genus Ganoderma

Native to several parts of Asia, including China, Korea, Japan, United States

Name Origin: Ling Zhi, which means 'Spirit Plant,' 'Ten Thousand Year Plant,' 'Mushroom Immortality,' 'Varnished Conk' because of its shiny appearance and 'Phantom Mushroom.

From the Latin name being, 'Ganoderma lucidum.' 'Gan means 'shiny.' Derm means 'skin.' Lucidum means 'brilliant.

Notes:

Often referred to frequently in ancient texts as the 'Mushroom of Immortality.'

First recorded over 2,000 years ago.

Around 200–250 CE, first reference was in Shénnóng Běncǎo Jīng's classic book, *Divine Farmer's Classic of Pharmaceutics.*

Revered by Buddhist monks, Taoists, Emperors, the Royalty of China, Korea, Japan, sages.

Boosts bees immune function as well as people.

If you dry mushrooms in the Sun, it increases their vitamin D content.

Beta glucans make up about 55% of Reishi's cells.

When harvesting Reishi, check the underside looking for white underneath. These mushrooms are young and contain the most medicinal compounds. Older Reishi's tend to be more bitter and tougher.

Parts used: whole mushroom

Curative Properties: adaptogenic, analgesic, antibacterial, anticancer, anticarcinogenic, antidiabetes, antidiabetic, antifatigue, antifungal, antihemorrhagic, antihypertensive, anti-inflammatory, antimicrobial, antineoplastic, antiosteoporosis, antioxidant, antiproliferative, antiviral, brain tonic, cardiac tonic, chemopreventive, hepatic, hepatoprotective, hypotensive, hypothyroidal, immune modulator, immunostimulant, lymphatic, neuro-protective, protects the DNA and blocks cell mutations, sedative, radio-protective, tonic, restorative, restores homeostasis

Energy and flavors: warm, sweet

Cautions:

1. Avoid if you're pregnant or breastfeeding, unless under medical supervision. There hasn't been much research done on the safety and long-term effects for these populations. Which means that there have not been many cases of anyone being injured by it.

2. Any type of bleeding disorder; upcoming surgeries; blood pressure medications, blood thinners, chemotherapy drugs or immunosuppressant medications; or have issues with blood clotting, ask your Healthcare Provider.

3. Please discontinue use or consult a Healthcare Provider if experiencing bloody stool.

Conditions: allergies, anxiety, asthma, autoimmune conditions, blood pressure (high), cancer, cholesterol (high), damaged blood vessels, decreased immune function, diabetes, depression, digestive problems, fatigue, flu, food allergies, frequent infections (bronchitis, urinary tract infections, etc.), heart disease, HIV/AIDS or hepatitis, hormonal imbalances, hypertension, infections (microbial, viral and fungal), inflammation, insomnia, leaky gut syndrome, liver disease, low energy, pain, skin disorders, sleep disorders, stomach ulcers, stress, thyroid disorder, tumor growth, urination (frequent), viruses

Bio chemical constituents: ergosterol, fumaric acid, amino glucose, mannitol; coumarins; alkaloids; lactose, various enzymes, triterpenes, amino acids, beta-glucans, plant sterols, polysaccharides

Polysaccharides: a water-soluble type of nutrient found in carbohydrate rich foods and are known to have antitumor abilities.

Parts of the body: cardiovascular, central nervous, digestive, endocrine systems, heart, immune, liver

Preparations~

****Because some of the active compounds that are present are not soluble in water such as the terpenes and sterols, a double extraction process is required with mushrooms. First an alcohol extraction, then a decoction to release any compounds not released into the alcohol extraction, such as the polysaccharides, beta glucans and proteoglycans. ****

Double Extraction Method Alcohol Tincture:

For mushrooms, alcohol is the preferred medium over glycerin…
Fill jar half way with dried mushroom.
Cover with organic grain alcohol.
Cap, label, shake every day infusing with healing intention, love and gratitude.
After 1 month, strain.

Decoction:

Take alcohol soaked mushrooms and process with this
extraction method~
Put mushrooms in pan and fill with twice the amount of water.
Bring to a boil, adding more water as it boils off.
Simmer for 2 hours-4 hours, the longer the better.
Let sit for 12 hours.

Remove mushrooms from liquid.
Add equal parts of alcohol tincture and decoction.
If you started with 100 proof alcohol, then your tincture will
be 25% alcohol.
Use as Supreme Immune Tonic

Dose:

Standard 3 to 5 gm a day
Although doses up to 15 gm are not uncommon for more serious illnesses.

Standard Dose:

½ teaspoon two or three times a day.
If drinking as a tea or taking in supplement form, it is suggested to be taken on an empty stomach for maximum effectiveness. To ensures proper absorption of the antioxidants and active ingredients, consume with water and vitamin C foods.

Recipes~

My Favorite Smoothie Recipe

Ingredients:
Juice - apple, peach, mango any one or all
Frozen fruit - cherries, blueberries, strawberries, mangoes, peaches
Bananas
3-5 droppers Reishi extract
Cottage cheese - 2 tbs. per person
Flaxseed oil - 2 tbs. per person
2-3 Cannabis/Hemp leaves
*Note: Raw Cannabis leaves contain THCA which cannot get you high, once it is heated, it is converted to THC which can get you high. This process is called Decarboxylation and requires a temperature of 200 degrees for the change to occur

Directions:
Blend cottage cheese and Flaxseed oil in blender first until creamy, this is crucial as blending them together is where the magic happens, then add your banana, juice, frozen fruit
Blend until desired consistency, if too thin, add more fruit, if too thick, add more juice

Dose: 8 oz. a day, but we like to drink 2 a day, one in the morning and one at night for dessert

Variations:
CBD Oil-a few drops can be added and stirred in at the end
Sometimes I like to put chocolate chips or cacao nibs
Other additions: Raspberries, blackberries, grape juice, cherry juice

Here's a lemonade recipe from Red Moon Herbs~

Long Life Reishi Lemonade Recipe

1/2 - 1 oz dried Reishi slices
6 cups water
1 - 2 cinnamon sticks
2 - 4 tbsp lemon juice

stevia, sugar, maple syrup, or honey to taste

Place your dried Reishi slices and cinnamon sticks in the water and bring to a boil. Simmer this mixture on low heat for one hour to even up to half a day or longer. The longer you simmer the mixture, the stronger the Reishi will become and the more of its beneficial components will be released.

Supreme Mushroom Soup Recipe for Immune Strengthening

Inspired by Herbalist, Juliet Blankespoor

Serves 6 making about 1 gallon

Ingredients:

½ oz. organic dried Shiitake mushrooms, cut into 1 in. piece
½ oz. organic dried Maitake mushrooms, cut into 1 in. pieces
1 slice organic Reishi mushroom
5-7 slices organic Astragalus
½ oz. organic Nori flakes
½ oz. of organic Kelp flakes
1 medium organic onion
1 large organic sweet potato
1 medium organic red potato
3 organic celery stalks
½ bunch asparagus
3 medium organic carrots
3 organic garlic cloves
3 tbsp. organic extra virgin olive oil
1 tsp. organic dried Rosemary leaves
1 tsp. organic dried Marjoram
1 tsp. organic dried Thyme
2 tsp. organic Chia seeds
1 tsp organic grated Ginger
2 cups organic vegetable broth
2 tsp. miso
2 qt. loosely packed, organic seasonal cooking greens such as Kale,
Collards, Spinach, Nettle, or Lamb's Quarters about 4 oz. by weight
1 cup fresh peas from the garden
4 tbs. nutritional yeast flakes

Coarsely ground organic black pepper, to taste
Organic tamari or sea salt, to taste
Organic parsley
Scallions to garnish

Directions:

Soak the mushrooms, Astragalus, Nori and Kelp in 4 cups of
water overnight, stored in the refrigerator.
The next day, add the soaked water, mushrooms, Nori and
Kelp into a large pot with an additional 5 ½ cups of water.
Cover and simmer for 1 hour.
Chop the onions, sweet potato, potato, celery, asparagus,
carrots, Ginger into 1-inch pieces.
Set aside.
Mince the garlic and set aside.
Warm the olive oil and sauté the onions for a few minutes until softened,
then add the chopped vegetables and peas except the garlic and continue
to sauté for ten minutes, continuously stirring. When the mushrooms
and Nori have simmered for one hour, add the sautéed vegetables, dried
herbs and vegetable broth to the mushroom-seaweed pot.

Simmer for another 15 to 20 minutes, until the root vegetables are soft.

Add the cooking greens and cook for a few minutes until tender, but still
green.

Turn off the heat and add salt or tamari, to taste, along with the minced
garlic, miso.

Remove the Astragalus and Reishi slices by hand. Garnish with fresh
parsley and scallions.

<u>More Information</u>: Nothing compares to mushroom energy, the
supreme deep immune system tonic nourishes the spirit, essence and vital
energy, remember when we learned about your Aura and Chakras? This
is one plant that penetrates through the layers, healing the energetic body
as well.

According to Dr. Axe: "Recent findings suggest that Reishi mushrooms
can lower inflammation and increase the release of natural killer cells,
which work to remove various types of mutated cells from the body. This

makes the Reishi mushroom ideal for preventing heart disease and working as a natural cancer treatment.

Some of the ways that Reishi mushrooms work to promote better health include:

- activating cytotoxic receptors (NKG2D/NCR)
- inhibiting cell proliferation
- suppressing vascular endothelial growth factor
- increasing plasma antioxidant capacity
- enhancing immune response
- converting excess testosterone to dihydrotestosterone"

Among only a handful of herbs nourishing all three of the foundational concepts of TCM, the three treasures: *Jing, Chi,* and *Shen.* Of all of the thousands of plants out there, only a handful's effects ripple through all of the energetic spheres, Reishi is one of them.

Considered the most supreme as a *Shen* tonic, *Shen* is our spirit, and/or our "higher consciousness," which represents the divine spark within all of us and the source of who we truly are. We must nourish and maintain *Shen* to lead a long and peaceful life.

Reishi is not a mushroom that we utilized regularly for my husband's healing journey to rid his body of cancer, but after watching *The Truth About Cancer* and learning about the supplement 7M from Organixx, which is a blend of 7 different healing mushrooms, it has been a supplement that we have utilized for his immune system maintaining optimum function, making his body inhospitable to cancer and ensuring that it does not return.

My daughter's ex husband used to collect Reishi's and sell them to a connection he had in Asia. It was very specific how he was to harvest, dry and ship them out.

Turkey Tail Mushroom

Growing On My Property That I Made A Tincture With

"Whether you use fungi to make a mushroom soup or as a remedy for someone dealing with cancer, whether you stir them up in a witch's cauldron of spiraling power or sew them into a spirit bag, mushrooms offer magic and mystery, good health and good cheer."

—*Susan Weed*

Turkey Tail Mushroom - *Coriolus Versicolor, Trametes*

Versicolor, Polyporus Versicolor, ThuZhi (China), Kawaritake (Japan)

In Cancer Free Protocol

Other names: Cloud Mushroom

Genus: Polypore Mushroom or Bracket Fungi meaning it forms thin, circular structures that appear leaf like, Basidiomycetes class of Fungi

Native to Europe, Asia, North America

Name Origin: derived from the resemblance to a turkey's tail

Notes:

The Chinese have been brewing it for thousands of years.

Used as early as the fifteenth century during the Ming Dynasty in China.

Spiritual attunement and affinity are associated with its cloud like image symbolizing them.

Egyptian Hieroglyphics referring to mushrooms as the 'plant of Immortality,' called the 'Sons of the Gods' sent to Earth on lightning bolts and eaten only by nobles and pharaohs.

One of the most researched mushrooms.

Drying mushrooms in the Sun increases their vitamin D content.

Parts used: whole mushroom

Curative Properties: adaptogen, antibacterial, anticancer, antidiarrhetic, antifungal, antihemorrhagic, antihypertensive, antiinflammatory, antimicrobial, antineoplastic, antioxidant, antitumor, antiulcer, antiviral, clear blockages, detoxifying, eliminate stagnation, hypothyroidal, immune booster, immune system modulator, immunostimulant, oxidation resistance, reducing blood fat, restorative

Energy and flavors: slightly cool, bland, neutral, sweet,

Cautions: none known, but always a good idea to check with your midwife or if you are pregnant or nursing.

Conditions: appetite (poor), cancer, chronic bronchitis, chronic fatigue, cirrhosis, common cold, cough, Crohn's disease, diabetes, flu, gum disease, hepatitis, HIV/AIDS, HPV (human papillomavirus), hyperlipidemia, hyperthyroidism (Grave's disease), IBS, immune weakness, indigestion, infection, inflammation, jaundice, leaky gut syndrome, loose bowels, lung disease, malaria, nephritis, oncovirus, oxidative stress, rheumatoid arthritis, stress, tinnitus, ulcerative colitis, virus infections

Bio chemical constituents: polysaccharide K (PSK), prebiotics, selenium, vitamin D, vitamin B3, beta glucans polysaccharide, proteins, amino acids, polysaccharopeptide (PSP), triterpenoids, ergosterols, sitosterols, coriolan, flavonoids quercetin and baicalein

Parts of the body: digestive tract, immune system, kidney, liver, lungs, spleen

Preparations~

****Because some of the active compounds that are present are not soluble in water such as the terpenes and sterols, a double extraction process is required with mushrooms. First an alcohol extraction, then a decoction to release any compounds not released into the alcohol extraction, such as the polysaccharides, beta glucans and proteoglycans.****

Double Extraction Method

Alcohol Tincture:

For mushrooms, alcohol is the preferred medium over
glycerin…
Fill jar half way with dried mushroom
Cover with organic grain alcohol
Cap, label, shake every day infusing with healing intention,
love and gratitude.
After 1 month, strain.

Decoction:

Place alcohol soaked mushrooms in a pot, cover with twice the
amount of water.
1 part chopped up mushroom
2 parts hot water using triple the amount of water used for the
tincture.
Simmer on low heat for 2 to 6 hours.
Water will reduce quite a bit
Cool, compost mushrooms.

Add equal parts decoction to equal parts alcohol tincture
giving you a 25% alcohol extract if the alcohol was 100 proof
(50% alcohol, 50% water)
Cap, shake well, label.
Standard Dose:
½ teaspoon 2 to 3 times a day

<u>More Information</u>: Turkey Tail was one of the first supplements that I started my husband on when we found out that we might be dealing with the 'C' word. But it wasn't my choice, it was his body who chose it when we were visiting a Kinesiolost in our area.

With a number of supplements offered to my husband, his body indicated that it wanted the Turkey Tail, finding the best source I could, I ordered it for him and he started taking it immediately along with a number of other supplements.

After two weeks, his symptoms had diminished so much that I didn't even want to go for the biopsy as it wasn't really an issue anymore. Anyone experiencing any kind of immune challenges should really research Turkey Tail, improving the gut microbiome, especially for those who have taken repeated doses of antibiotics.

Turkey Tail nourishes the gut and intestinal tract replacing vital microorganisms that antibiotics destroy. Being as 80% of your immune system is in your gut, having that beneficial flora in the proper balance is vital to optimum immune function. Improving the absorption of nutrients like vitamins D and B12. Sometimes being referred to as your second brain, the bacteria in your gut plays a crucial role in the proper functioning of most of body systems.

I hope you have enjoyed the Mushroom Profiles and now if you're interested in the technical actions of the mushrooms, please see Appendix A below…

More beautiful mushrooms I found!

Appendix A

Actions Of Mushrooms~

-Adaptogens restore homeostasis within the body balancing hormones, lowering cortisol levels, produce positive stress response, increase recovery time after an illness and immune building function. According to a Russian Dr., I.I. Brekhmann, who popularized the concept of adaptogens through his research, there are 3 criteria that they must fulfill:

1. Do no harm, place no stress on the body

2. Assist the body in adapting to a wide range of internal stressors (emotions, noise, pollution) as well as environmental ones

3. Has an amphoteric (normalizing) effect on the activity of several body systems--especially the nervous system, hormonal system, and immune system

Indications: stress, hormone imbalances, pain, illness stress include impatience, anxiety, irritability, sleep, poor diet

Herbs: Chaga, Reishi, Turkey Tail

-Analgesic, Anodyne

-Analgesics reduce pain. Direct application externally or can be taken internally, depending on the injury

Indications: pain, injuries, inflammation, joint pains, arthritis, neck and back pain, tendonitis

Herbs: Reishi

-Antiallergics counteract allergies. Herbs possessing anti-inflammatory and antihistamine effects on the body.

Indications: allergies

Herbs: Chaga

-Antibacterial herbs fight and destroy bacteria. Many herbs that contain essential oils are antibacterial and antiseptic and some of the most effective herbs contain berberine.

Indications: bacterial infections

Herbs: Chaga, Turkey Tail

-Anticoagulants (coumarin-containing plants and salicylate containing plants), also known as blood thinners, delaying or preventing clots, mildly inhibiting blood coagulation through platelet activity. Substitute for daily aspirin therapy

Indications: blood clots, strokes, heart conditions, Angina, hepatitis, coronary artery disease, dysmenorrhea, rheumatoid arthritis, traumatic injury, tumors, depression, renal failure, stroke prevention and post-stroke syndrome, anti-edema

Herbs: Chaga

-Antidiarrhetics slow or stop diarrhea

3 Mechanisms are used:

Bulking agents~Mucilage is a type of soluble fiber that absorbs water and forming a semi-solid gel. Act as bulking agents providing better consistency to the stool decreasing urgency, giving better bowel control, reducing water loss

Astringents~suppress diarrhea with Tannins that bind to proteins on the bowel walls altering the permeability, reducing water loss. Also increasing the intestines resistance to infections by reducing the binding of micro-organism and their enterotoxins to the bowel walls. Used to stop internal bleeding associated with dysentery.

Antisecretory~Secretory diarrhea occurs when water absorption is impaired and excess water is pumped into the bowels. According to Matt Gowan, BSC, ND, 'water follows the movement of salt (sodium, potassium) in the body. Sodium & potassium are actively pumped from the bowels to increase water absorption thereby hydrating the body. Conversely chlorine ions being secreted into the bowels lead to sodium and thus water loss to hydrate stool but in extreme cases cause diarrhea.

The involvement of chlorine transporters (CaCC, CFTR) with diarrhea is supported by research.[1] Some antisecretory herbs for diarrhea reduce diarrhea by inhibiting chlorine transporter (e.g. CaCC) and they may also affect the absorption of sodium or potassium.'

Indications: diarrhea, loose stool

Herbs: Turkey Tail

- Antifungal inhibits or retards growth of pathogenic fungus

Indications: Candida, Thrush, fungal infections

Herbs: Chaga, Reishi, Turkey Tail

-Anti-inflammatories reduce swelling, lower inflammation, either by inhibiting prostaglandin (local-acting hormones) synthesis or

blocking the production of inflammatory substances (such as histamine) by the immune system, or by other means.

Herbs: Chaga, Reishi, Turkey Tail

-Antihemorrhagic (also known as hemostatic) are powerful astringents that arrest mild bleeding

Indications: bleeding

Herbs: Reishi

-Anti-microbial herbs destroy or resist pathogenic microorganisms such as bacteria, fungi, or protozoans by killing or inhibiting their growth and multiplication.

Indications: infections, wounds, sores

Herbs: Chaga, Turkey Tail

-Antineoplastic (anticancer) herbs destroy, inhibit or prevent the maturation and proliferation of neoplasms (tumors) that may become malignant. Tumor reducing properties.

Indications: tumors, cancer, growths

Herbs: Chaga, Turkey Tail

-Antioxidants fight free radicals, counteracting the negative effects of oxidation on body tissues. According to Christopher Hobbs- 'Antioxidants are compounds such as phenolic compounds found in fruits that bind with "free-radicals" and deactivate them. Free-radicals are

highly reactive molecules containing oxygen that can bind with the cell-walls and genetic material in the body's healthy cells, disrupting their function or even destroying them.

Free-radical damage in the body is associated with an increased risk of cancer and is the main mechanism by which our vital organs are damaged when they do not receive sufficient blood, or when there is an infection.

For instance, in a heart attack, the heart muscle is deprived of blood for a period of time, and extensive damage to the heart muscle can occur-- much of this damage involves the action of free-radicals, according to some scientists.'

Indications: oxidative stress, premature aging, wrinkles, age spots, heart disease

Herbs: Chaga, Turkey Tail

-Antivirals kill viruses

Indications: Candida, HIV/AIDS, colds, viral infections, virus'

Herbs: Chaga, Turkey Tail

-Blood Purifiers are detoxifying and neutralizing acids in the blood and lymph nodes, too, rich in Folic Acid, Vitamins A and C, polysaccharides, beta-carotene, antioxidants, supporting and stimulating the liver and gall bladder functions

Indications: cancer, infections, leukemia, blood borne diseases, Hepatitis, HIV/AIDS, anemia, illness, chronic disease, Herxheimer Effect

Herbs: Chaga, Reishi

-Brain Tonics oxygenate the brain, increase concentration, improve memory, enhance focus, clear mental fog, increase neurotransmitter communication

Indications: Alzheimers, Dementia, Parkinson's, Huntington's, brain fog, chemo brain, memory loss, inability to focus, unable to concentrate

Herbs: Reishi

-Cardiac tonics effect the heart, benefiting the cardiovascular system

Indications: Angina, irregular heartbeat, heart conditions or disease, oppression over pyloric valve

Herbs: Reishi

-Decoction extraction of herbal material made through boiling or simmering of water, usually a long simmer (20-45 minutes). Preferred method for denser plant parts such as roots, bark, seeds, berries and mushrooms. Decoctions are more concentrated than infusions.

-Expectorants loosen and expel mucus from the nose, throat and lungs. For productive phlegm producing coughs

Antitussives (cough suppressants) for dry coughs, may be indicated to suppress the body's urge to cough.

Indications: Asthma, bronchial congestion, coughs, respiratory conditions

Herbs: Chaga

-Hepatics aid the liver by detoxifying, strengthening and toning it, increases the flow of bile from the liver, regulating it's action

Indications: Hepatitis, headaches, poor digestion, PMS, jaundice

Herbs: Reishi, Turkey Tail

-Hypotensives reduce elevated blood pressure, resulting in low blood pressure, resembling actions of a antihypertensive which is an agent that lowers blood pressure. May require several months of use to have noticeable effects for some.

Indications: high blood pressure (hypertension)

Herbs: Chaga

-Hypothyroidals reduce the thyroxin output of the thyroid gland

Indications: hyperthyroidism, overactive thyroid, Rapid heart rate and palpitations, Goiter (swelling of the thyroid gland)Shortness of breath, reddened, swollen, and bulging eyes (in Graves disease), shakiness, tremors, heat intolerance, sweating, occasionally, raised, thickened skin over back, back of feet, hands, shins, face even, moist skin, increased perspiration, increase in appetite accompanied by weight loss, irritability, difficulty concentrating, possible delirium, insomnia, crisis: panic, very rapid pulse fever, agitation, anxious, menstrual irregularity

Herbs: Reishi, Turkey Tail

-Immunomodulators modulate the immune system with a slightly milder effect, many of these herbs are adaptogens, restoring balance wherever needed

Indications: weakened immune function, cancer,

Herbs: Chaga, Reishi, Turkey Tail

-Immunostimulant actions include increasing white blood cells, increasing available energy in the body, removing blockages, removing causes of diminished immune function, improving circulation, detoxing the liver, eliminating factors contributing to increased stress levels, lowering stress levels, lowering cortisol and adrenaline levels, improving digestion, absorption and bioavailability of nutrients, purifying the blood.

Not recommended for continued use without a break in between cycles, use for short cycles (up to 10 days on 3 days off) for people who are not immuno-compromised, can be contraindicated for people suffering from severely compromised immunity.

Some risks involving overstimulation of an immune system that has no reserves, actually leading to immune suppression

Indications: cancer, suppressed immune function, chronic sickness, colds, flus, sore throat

Herbs: Reishi Mushroom, Turkey Tail

-Lymphatics stimulating lymphatic system, removing blockages, eliminating toxins, increasing lymph function

Indications: swollen lymph nodes, cancer, illness, Lymphoma, Leukemia, blood diseases

Herbs: Reishi

-Pectorals strengthen and heal respiratory system

Indications: bronchitis, Pneumonia

Herbs: Chaga

-Restoratives (Tonics) restore balance and vitality to the body and its systems

Indications: imbalance, disease, illness

Herbs: Chaga, Reishi, Turkey Tail